Free Climbing with John Bachar

Free Climbing with John Bachar

John Bachar and Steve Boga

STACKPOLE
BOOKS

Published by
STACKPOLE BOOKS
5067 Ritter Road
Mechanicsburg, PA 17055

Printed in the United States of America

10 9 8 7 6 5 4 3 2 1

First edition

Cover photo by John McDonald

Cover design by Kathleen D. Peters

Illustrations by Thomas Aubrey

Library of Congress Cataloging-in-Publication Data

Bachar, John.
    Free climbing with John Bachar / John Bachar and Steve Boga. —
1st ed.
      p. cm.
    ISBN 0-8117-2517-0
    1. Rock climbing. I. Boga, Steve, 1947- . II. Title.
GV200.2.B33 199695-50948
796.5'223—dc20
                                                95-50948
                                                  CIP

Contents

An Important Note to Readers

This book contains much useful information about the sport of rock climbing. Before engaging in this potentially hazardous sport, however, you must do more than read a book.

The sport requires skill, concentration, physical strength and endurance, proper equipment, knowledge of fundamental principles and techniques, and unwavering commitment to your own safety and that of your companions.

The publisher and authors obviously cannot be responsible for your safety. Because rock climbing entails the risk of serious and even fatal injury, we emphasize that you should not begin climbing except under expert supervision. No book can substitute for proper training and experience under the guidance and supervision of a qualified teacher.

Introduction

The purpose of this book is to present free-climbing techniques that will enable newer climbers to meet the challenges that rock offers. If you apply these techniques to natural geologic formations—faces, cracks, holds—you may just find that you're a climber.

Of course, by newer climbers I don't mean absolute beginners. Novices should not try to rely solely on this book to start free climbing. Take a class or go out with an experienced friend, then use this book as an adjunct to fill in the blanks or clarify arcane information.

A lot of the technique information may be rather bewildering to novices. Bounce new ideas gleaned from the second and third chapters off that experienced friend or instructor. I also suggest that you study the glossary first and refer to it later, which will help you talk the talk.

And finally, be aware of the importance of safety and proper equipment when you're learning to climb. Although I've given it short shrift in this book, that doesn't mean it's not important. I haven't stayed alive and healthy through almost two decades of climbing by ignoring personal safety. To learn more about those two critical subjects, refer to the first book in this series: *Aid Climbing with Mike Corbett*. Even if you have no desire to be an aid climber, Mike Corbett can teach you about rock-climbing equipment and safety techniques that will serve you well in free climbing.

I've tried to convey the techniques of free climbing as I have learned and practiced them in twenty-five years of climbing and teaching. I've also included tips on training, practice, injuries, and their rehabilitation. I've even gone on a bit about ethics, a subject on which I have strong feelings.

If you stay with it, you'll discover rock that no one has ever climbed before. And instead of seeing blank rock, you'll start to see edges, pockets, smear bumps—holds one and all.

Knock yourself out!

— 1 —

History of Free Climbing

Such beauty . . . turns satisfaction to pure joy.
—JOHN HARLIN

Climbing is natural, and early man was a climber out of necessity, usually to escape predators or chase down food. Native Americans, Africans, Thais, Tibetans, and many others have climbed for millennia, but it was not until the eighteenth century that Europeans started climbing for sport. Back then, the summit was the be-all and end-all of the climb. It mattered not a whit *how* one made it to the top, only that one made it. Whether it was a scramble that required no equipment or a roped climb, a party's means of achieving success were not questioned.

In the 1920s, a rating system was developed in Germany by climber Willo Welzenbach, and by 1937 Sierra Club climbers in the United States had pretty much adopted the German rating system. At this time, U.S. climbers were focused on meeting the challenges of climbing the biggest cliffs around, regardless of style, aid or free. Such climbs as the Nose of El Capitan were the main goals for this generation.

The learning curve was steeper in Europe. While U.S. climbers were still struggling with 5.7, climbers in Dresden, Germany, had free climbed 5.10 b/c (by present YDS rating).

Eventually, U.S. climbers realized that given enough time and bolts, any wall could be climbed. They began to concentrate on style rather than summit. Free climbing, which initially meant "free of aid" climbing, became the main focus for climbers after the golden age of

1

Yosemite big-wall aid climbing had seen many of the world's major faces conquered.

At first, U.S. free climbs were identified only as easy, moderate, or advanced. Later, Royal Robbins and climbing partner Don Wilson separated Class 5 (free climbing) into ten subcategories (5.0 to 5.9), with 5.0 the easiest, 5.5 moderate, and 5.9 the most difficult free climb then done.

This decimal system was accepted and adopted by the rest of California and, eventually, the United States. It reached Yosemite around 1956 and later became known as the Yosemite Decimal System (YDS).

In 1952 Royal Robbins stunned the U.S. climbing community, such as it was, by climbing the "Open Book" route at Tahquitz Rock without direct aid. It was the first 5.9 in America and, as such, the hardest free climb in the country.

In 1957 Ray Northcutt climbed the Bastille crack direct start, the first 5.10 lead (now 5.10d), in Eldorado Canyon, Colorado.

As free climbers improved their skills, the YDS had to expand to accommodate ever more difficult climbs. It has grown to include, as of this writing, 5.14d, with climbs 5.10 through 5.14 further subdivided into a, b, c, and d.

In 1961 Chuck Pratt and his partner free-climbed the "Crack of Doom" at Elephant Rock in Yosemite. Pratt's bold lead was in its own class for several years.

During the 1960s free climbers began applying their skills to the big walls in Yosemite. By 1970 Jim Bridwell was one of the driving forces on the free-climbing scene. Big Jim created classic routes with names like "Gripper" (5.10), "Butterfingers" (5.11), and "Outer Limits" (5.10).

In 1975 Ron Kauk and I free-climbed "Hot Line" on Elephant Rock, one of the first 5.12s in the United States. That same year, Kauk, John Long, and I free-climbed the east face of Washington Column, renaming it "Astro Man." This was the most sustained free climb in Yosemite and is still considered one of the best free climbs in the world. Our group would dominate the free-climbing scene for the next decade, setting standards wherever we climbed.

A lthough free-climbing ratings vary from one country to another, the Yosemite Decimal System translates pretty well wherever you are in the United States. A climb in the Shawangunks similar to a 5.9 Yosemite will also be rated 5.9. It's important that the rating system be fairly consistent, so that climbers can rely on guidebooks and avoid climbs way beyond their skills.

Lynn Hill, who has long been the best female rock climber in the world, says that "difficulty depends on the steepness of the rock, size of holds, how hard they are to hang on to, how far apart they are, the kind of movements they require, if you have to jump to holds, how many holds there are before you get to a resting place, and how hard it is to stop and put in protection."

– 2 –

Face-Climbing Technique

There are three basic categories of rock faces: less than vertical (a slab), vertical, and more than vertical (an overhang). Weight distribution, body positioning, and the balance between use of hands and feet change according to the steepness of the rock.

On a rock that's less than vertical, the most common beginner mistake is leaning into the rock. Try to keep your weight over your feet as much as possible; this will enable you to maintain the greatest amount of friction between your feet and the rock. The more you lean in, the less friction you create.

As a face gets steeper, less of a climber's body weight is supported by feet and more by hands. Still, you should use your feet as much as possible to alleviate the burden on your arms. When the rock is vertical, lean in just enough to support your weight with your feet, but not enough to restrict your view of the rock or your movement.

When the rock is more than vertical, your arms take the brunt of the weight, but the selection of footholds is just as important. Your feet should be positioned to control the direction of the forces placed on your arms and fingers.

In face climbing, there are fewer technique components for the hands and feet than in crack climbing; rather, it's more about body position: What kind of body position will enable your to reach the next hold?

Common handholds: a knob...   A pocket...

An edge...

A slope.

Hand Technique

Hand technique involves using features as handholds—that is, holding on to knobs, pockets, edges, or slopes. In general, there are two ways to grab edges with the fingers: *crimping* and *open-hand techniques*.

Crimping. Crimping involves grabbing a hold so that the fingers are in a scrunched-up position. Usually it's necessary to crimp the worst holds, like small "dime edges" and incut flakes. Crimping requires more strength, stresses the tendons of the hands more, and puts them at greater risk for injury than using open-hand techniques.

Open-Hand Techniques. If you face a little larger, or positive, edge, open-hand the hold, as that lets more of the skeletal system of the hand bear the brunt. Grab on as if it were a chin-up bar or the rung of a ladder, with an open, relaxed hand.

One open-hand technique is *palming*, in which you put your entire palm, or maybe the last three knuckles, straight on the rock. This technique is used on bigger holds or slopes. It relies on the friction between the rock and the skin of the palm. It can be a tenuous hold, because if you move your hand slightly and break the friction, you may start sliding. This is because dynamic friction is less than static friction—once something is moving, it takes less force to keep it moving than it did

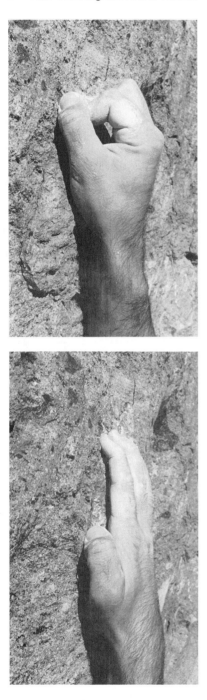

Crimping a small edge.

(*Below left*) An open-hand hang on a small finger edge.
(*Below right*) An open-hand grab of a two-finger pocket.

Palming a sloping hold.

to break it from its static position. The trick is to prevent such move-ment in the first place.

These hand techniques are not always used with a downward pull. At times it is necessary to use side pulls (inward to outward force, or vice versa) or even upward pulls, depending on body position and the move being attempted.

Whether you are forced to crimp or are able to use an open-hand technique, always conserve energy and never pull harder than you have to.

Foot Technique

Proper foot technique is critical when face-climbing. Slab climbing generally requires smearing techniques, vertical climbing requires edging techniques, and overhang climbing requires techniques that use creative positioning of the feet.

Smearing. Smearing is used on slopes that lack definite edges. Place your foot on the part of the rock that slopes the least, laying as much sole rubber onto the rock as possible. Distribute your weight over as much surface area of the boot as you can. That's smearing.

Heel hooking can be like having a third arm.

This technique isn't really new to you; you use it whenever you walk up a slight hill. It's just a matter of spreading your weight over a large area and making maximum use of the static friction created by the rubber sole against the rock.

Edging. Edging is done by butting the edge of your boot onto a rock edge. Imagine trying to stand on a miniature shelf with the edge of your boot. You may use the front edge of your boot, the inside edge by the big toe, the outside edge, or even the heel.

Other Foot Techniques. In between smearing and edging, there are a lot of holds that aren't quite either. Maybe we should call the techniques needed for those holds *smedging*.

There are other creative ways to use your feet, such as *heel hooking*, a rarely used but sometimes effective technique. Heel hooking is an attempt to use the foot as a hand. You hook the heel of your boot over or behind a flake, knob, corner, shelf, or any feature that will accom-

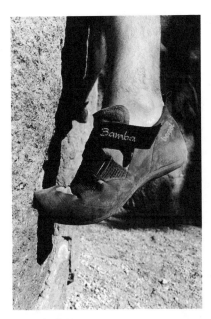

Frontal edging.   Inside edging.

modate such a move. Often it means raising your foot over your head and hooking it over a ledge. You can sometimes use heel hooks on larger holds, maneuvering the leg almost as a third arm.

A similar technique is the *toe hook*. On overhangs, you may be able to use the toe of your boot the way you would use your fingers in an upward pull.

There may be times when you can get only one foot on a hold. It may be advantageous to leave the other foot dangling, or you might want to use a *rand smear*, pushing into the side of the rock with the side of your boot.

Body Position

Crack climbing is usually quite linear, with straight-line body positioning. But in face climbing you have to decide among a wide variety of holds, to the left, right, or above, and then maneuver your body into advantageous positions to help you make reaches. Sometimes your legs and arms are splayed out like a starfish.

You will use several common body positions over and over again to make reaches. Let's look at some reach-enabling positions.

The one-arm lock-off allows you to make a lot of other moves on the rock.

One-Arm Lock-Off. The one-arm lock-off is a basic technique that allows you to make a lot of other moves on the rock. Pull up as high as you can and lock off one arm while releasing the other arm to reach for a new hold. Pull yourself high enough that your hand is next to your shoulder; this offers a distinct mechanical advantage over, say, a half-bent position. Getting the hand in close to the shoulder will enable you to use your upper-back muscles, which tend to be very strong, and will enable you to reach farther than you otherwise could. This technique can be applied to both face and crack climbing.

Opposite-Hand, Opposite-Foot Lock-Off. The opposite-hand, opposite-foot lock-off is a powerful position allowing you to make the reach with only two points of contact with the rock. Let's say that you've found a good right handhold and left foothold, and now you want to reach straight up, or up and left. Pull up so that your right shoulder is even with your right hand, lock off, then reach for the new hold with your left hand. Since you need only one foothold instead of two, you save time and therefore strength.

Backstep Reach. The backstep reach is another opposite-hand, opposite-foot technique. Here you need a handhold directly above a

The backstep reach is a good move for long reaches.

Manteling is a multi-step move most often used in bouldering.

foothold. It's harder to find the right alignment of holds necessary for this maneuver, but when you do, you can make a big reach pretty easily. Let's say you have a handhold with your right hand, while your right foot is edging on a foothold below. Use the strength of your leg to push yourself up until the handhold is chest high, then lock off, twist your body, and reach with the other hand. The twist allows you to reach higher than you ordinarily would. The backstep reach can also be used for underclings and inverse holds. Some of the longest reaches you can make are from a backstep out of an undercling.

Manteling. Manteling is usually used to pull up onto a ledge when no reachable handholds are available. First use your arms to pull up chest high. Then lock off with one arm and place the heel of the other hand on the ledge, with the fingers pointing inward toward the other hand and the chest. Cock the elbow up into a vertical position, as though you were going to support your weight with that arm. Now do the same thing with the other arm, so that both elbows are cocked up. Push up with both arms and straighten them, much like pushing up from a dip on the parallel bars. Carefully bring one foot up, squat, and transfer your weight onto that foot. Balance yourself and press up to a standing position to complete the move.

Although manteling is more common in bouldering, practice it in case you need it on a climb. In extreme cases, you may have to do a one-arm mantle, which, although more strenuous, follows the same steps as a two-arm mantle.

Figure-Four Reach. The figure-four reach is a wild, rarely used move that also can be done in a crack. Let's say you have a great right handhold or jam, and your right foot is pushing into the rock with a straight leg. Take your left leg and throw it over the top of your right arm, with the back of the left knee up against the inside of the right elbow. When you pull up like that and use the leg and buttocks muscles, you can reach quite high with the left hand.

Lynn Hill did the first female free climb of Choucas in Buoux. It's a very hard climb—a 5.13c, I believe. It has a classic dynamic section, requiring a lunge, that she did static by using a figure four. Some of the French climbers claimed she cheated, but that's ridiculous. The fact is, a dozen of the best climbers in the world hadn't thought of using the technique, even though they were aware of it.

– 3 –

Crack-Climbing Technique

There are three basic types of cracks: straight-in, dihedral, and flakes. *Straight-in cracks* (see finger lock photos, page 19) run perpendicular to the plane of the climbing surface. They can be slightly flared or even more defined at the lip.

Dihedrals (see finger lock figure, page 20) are shaped like open books. Sometimes the "pages" form a 90-degree angle, but not always; they can be more or less open. They can also be left- or right-facing. If the crack is parallel to the right face, then it is a right-facing dihedral.

Flakes are thinner plates of rock that appear to be plastered onto the main body of rock. They can be knife-edged, square-edged, or rounded.

Jams

To talk crack climbing is to talk jams. Many climbing techniques, such as pulling up on holds, placing feet for balance, or manteling, are pretty obvious. Jams, however, are a lot less obvious. At first it will seem unnatural to stick a finger or a hand in a crack and hang from it, but after you've mastered the technique, it's very effective. A good hand jam is one of the most secure holds a climber can have—more secure than grabbing a rung on a ladder. It can allow you to rest the other arm, arrange protection, apply chalk, and pull yourself up the rock.

Jams are classified by width (thin crack, wide crack, chimney) and/or the body part that is used to jam (finger crack, hand crack, fist

A flake.

crack). Because climbers come in different sizes, this is a subjective measurement; one person's hand jam may be another's fist jam.

Finger Locks. There are basically two kinds of finger locks, or jams: first knuckle and second knuckle. The thinnest jam is a first-knuckle finger lock. If a crack is too thin to accept a first knuckle, a jam is not possible, and you'll have to do something else. Sometimes with little pockets, you can get a finger-tip lock, which is not really a true lock. Without actually wedging a knuckle into a given pocket or crack, you lose the mechanical advantage that a finger lock offers.

In a typical finger lock, you insert at least your first knuckle into a crack, then slide it from a wide part down to a narrow, constricting

(*Above left*) **A thumb-up first-knuckle lock.**
(*Above right*) **Setting a thumb-down finger lock.**
(*Left*) **Weighting a thumb-down finger lock.**

part, until it sets like a stopper or a hex. Once it's set, you can pull up or out on it with little use of strength.

For slightly larger cracks, maybe ³/₄ inch wide, depending on your

Finger locking in a right-facing dihedral: thumb up and thumb down.

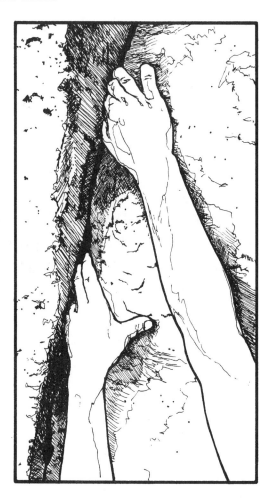

finger size, you can insert your finger to the second knuckle and slide it down until it sets.

A finger lock can be executed thumb up or thumb down. A really good constriction can be jammed thumb up, but a more parallel crack lacking constriction will probably have to be jammed thumb down, the more common position. As you pull on the thumb-down jam, you twist the wrist in a downward motion, causing your elbow to twist down and adding a torque factor that helps compensate for the lack of constriction.

The angle of the crack often dictates whether it should be jammed thumb up or thumb down. For example, if you confront a right-facing dihedral (with the crack parallel to the right wall of the dihedral), you may have to take it thumb up with your bottom right hand and thumb down with your top left hand.

Off-Finger Cracks. Slightly bigger cracks may be off-finger cracks. If you can get your finger in the crack past the second knuckle but can't get the third knuckle in, you have an off-finger crack. This kind of crack is too wide for a finger lock but too narrow for a hand jam. There are a couple of ways to approach this problem, although neither of them feels as secure as a finger lock.

The most common approach is finger stacking, in which the fingers are slightly offset, creating a stairlike look. The skin folds up and catches in the crack. This technique almost always requires a thumb-

Finger stacking.

Thumb stacking.

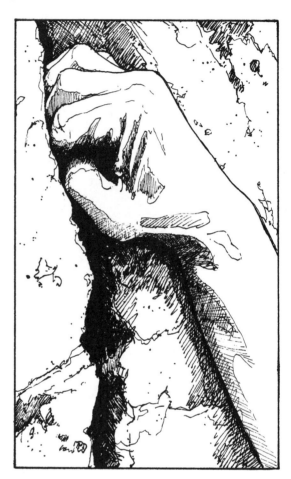

down approach; since there are no constrictions to catch your knuckles, you must count on the torque of the twisting elbow, which in turn twists the fingers, clumping them into the crack.

The second approach is thumb stacking, another thumb-down technique. Stick your thumb in the crack and find a constriction. Then place your fingers in the crack, allowing them to slide down on top of the thumb, like opposing stoppers. Your elbow, when weighted, will twist down, adding torque and a little security. Let the thumb float up, while weighting the jam with the first finger only. This is an insecure technique that takes a lot of practice to perfect. As a result, the off-finger crack is the worst type of thin crack to deal with.

Thin Hand Jams. As the crack widens further, it necessitates a thin hand jam. Here, the third knuckle, and maybe part of the palm, can enter the crack. The thin hand jam also demands a thumb-down approach. Stick your hand in and flex it as much as possible, using your palm muscles. This causes your hand to expand against the sides of the crack. In a true thin hand crack, you don't have many palm muscles available; instead, you must count on the torque provided by your elbow as you pull down on the jam.

With a thin hand jam, make short moves, pulling no more than a foot or two, maybe to chin level. Ideally, your hands should be between your chin and the top of your head. If you try to pull higher than that, you will no longer be creating additional torque with your elbow.

A good hand jam allows you to make use of most of the palm muscles.

Ordinary Hand Jams. The best hand jams are usually in cracks 1½ to 2 inches wide, into which you can fit the lower palm, making available more of the palm muscles. A true hand jam, this can be taken thumb up or thumb down. Unlike a finger jam, you don't need a constriction in the crack to work a hand jam; a parallel crack will do. In both constricting and parallel cracks, the basic technique is the same. You flex the palm muscles to expand the hand against the sides of the crack and create a secure hold. In a constriction, if you don't flex and expand the palm, you are just locking your wrist in the constriction, which is ineffective and painful.

The most common mistake with a hand jam is trying to bend the hand at the third knuckle in the belief that you are somehow creating a bridge between the base of the palm and the fingertips. This technique is insecure. Your hand is going to slide, cutting your skin. Instead, keep your hand straight, flexing the muscles in the palm and the back of the hand.

Here's an exercise to help you get used to the proper hand jam motion: Take your straight hand and open all the fingers, like a starfish. Then press the fingers tightly together side by side. It's especially important to bring the thumb hard against the first finger, causing the big thumb muscle to flex. Keeping the hand nearly straight, make a slight cup shape with the palm.

When it's time to set the jam, put your hand in the crack and, before flexing it, find the narrowest part of the crack. The hand should already feel resistance from the sides. When it's flexed, it expands against the sides of the crack, creating an expansion lock. Once those palm muscles are set, you should be able to wiggle your fingers without affecting the security of the hand jam. Hand jams are really a trick of muscle isolation in the palms.

If it's a perfect hand-size crack, try to take it thumb up, which allows you to move farther off the jam. If it's less than ideal, or if the crack is in a dihedral, facing left or right, you may have to go thumb down. If the jam is a little thinner, and you can't get your palm muscles all the way in the crack, you will probably need to take it thumb down.

The direction the crack leans, body positioning, and other factors will dictate the correct approach. Eventually, through practice and experimentation, you will intuitively know which approach to take before you even put your hand in the crack.

Wide Hand Jams. With cracks wider than about 2 inches—but not big enough for fist jamming—you have to use the somewhat insecure wide hand jam. If the crack is slightly too wide for your unflexed hand to be snug, you may have to bend or cup the hand at the third knuckle, which would ordinarily be undesirable. You are now using both a bend and a flex to expand the profile of your hand and create a bridge. This technique is usually done thumb up; thumb down, it's harder to cup the hand and you don't get much help from elbow torque. Even

A fist jam.

done thumb up, you won't make any long moves off this jam. Confine yourself to short, shufflelike movements.

Fist Jams. The first jam is used for cracks about 3 to 3½ inches, depending on your hand size. Make a loose fist, with the thumb on the outside of the fingers, and insert it in the crack. Try to place it so that you feel a little compression just from the tightness of the location. When you squeeze your fist tighter, the palm muscles below the pinkie expand against the sides of the crack and create a secure jam.

Experiment with this expansion by squeezing and relaxing, squeezing and relaxing. Feel the size difference between the tight fist and the limp fist. There should be about ½ inch difference. It may not seem like much, but it can be sufficient to create a secure jam.

Fist jams can be taken thumb up or thumb down, depending on your body position and whether the crack is straight in or a left or right dihedral. You can determine by trial and error whether the fist should be thumb up or thumb down. For example, on a right-facing flared dihedral (with the crack going to the left), you may have to take the crack with your left fist thumb up and your right fist thumb down, and shuffle up with short moves.

Foot Jams. So far we've focused on hand techniques for cracks up to fist size. Now let's see what the feet are doing. In all cracks, with the possible exception of chimneys, you'll need to use foot jams. Foot-jamming techniques vary from toe jams in finger-size cracks to heel-toe jams for off-width cracks.

Let's say the crack is a straight-in hand crack. Bend one leg at the knee, and bring your foot up toward your other knee so that the sole of the boot is vertical, as though you were trying to look at the bottom of your boot. That's the starting position for the basic foot jam. Your foot now has a narrower profile, allowing you to stick it farther into the crack than you could if your sole were perpendicular to the crack.

The biggest and most secure foot jam is a *heel-toe jam,* in which your foot is turned so that the toe is touching one side of the crack and the heel is touching the other. The key to a good foot jam is the twisting motion of the knee toward the center of the body, which creates a powerful torque effect with the foot. In a hand crack, your foot may go in as far as the arch. In a thin hand crack, your foot may go in only as far as your toes. This jam is harder to stand on, so try to gain security with the twisting motion. With even thinner cracks, you may have to search for a little pod or pocket that will accept at least the very tips of your toes. Here you're still relying on foot torque.

The heel-toe jam is very secure in this off-width crack.

Here are the two most important rules in jamming:

1. *Move one limb at a time.* Achieve solid jams or locks with three limbs before you move a fourth one. Avoid the bad habit of resting on one foot jam and one hand jam while maneuvering for a second hand jam. That dangling second foot doesn't help.

2. *Never move on a jam you can't hang on.* Never! Take the time to get the jam right, so that you know you can hang on it. In a typical bad scenario, a climber has one bombproof hand jam when he sets a second jam. The second jam feels okay, but as he moves on it, he realizes he can't hang on that second jam. The best he can do is retreat on the first jam and reset the second one.

Here's a story that illustrates the danger of moving on a tenuous jam: One time I was climbing at Joshua Tree with the late John Yablonsky. He decided he wanted to solo "More Monkey than Funky," a pretty stout 5.11a hand crack in a roof that had never been soloed. It was about 100 degrees F., and I suggested he wait until it was cooler, but he was adamant.

It was about a three-body-length roof crack, and he was hand-jamming vertically into the roof. At the lip of the roof, there were thin hand jams. He was getting thumb-down jams with the palm going in about halfway.

He got to where his feet were right at the lip and pulled up onto a new jam. He belatedly realized that this jam wasn't too good, but by changing position, he had made the first jam worse. So now he had two jams, neither of which was good enough to hang from. He couldn't take the top hand out and go back down and reset, and he couldn't take the bottom hand out.

He was 35 feet up, above some boulders. I was watching from below, and it occurred to me that this guy might be going to the hospital or the cemetery. It was only a matter of a couple of minutes before his muscles would blow out and he'd fall.

There was nothing he could do, and he knew it. He started moaning and crying, like someone about to be executed. Desperate, he spotted a wide, flared slot in the rock about 2 feet above his head. It was a tricky jam to execute, even if reached statically with enough time to set the jam properly.

In a last-ditch effort, he threw a dyno into the flare. But it didn't catch, and he started sliding down the flare. Finally, in the last inch, his skin latched onto the lip of the rock, stopping him.

I've never seen anyone else come that close to eating it.

Off-Width Cracks

Off-width cracks are too wide for a fist jam, so you will not be able to use the jamming techniques given thus far. Climbing off-width cracks—from slightly larger than a fist to wide enough to accommodate your sideways chest—is a challenge, a true test of technique. Scaling an off-width demands using all four limbs in harmony. A mistake with any one limb on an off-width can spell failure.

An arm bar is quite useful in a small off-width crack.

The smallest off-width—wider than a fist and thinner than a knee—can be a real challenge. If you can't do a fist jam and you can't quite fit a knee in the crack, you are forced to rely on the classic off-width technique, using arm bars for the upper body and foot jams for the feet. An arm bar is a technique in which the open hand presses against one side of the crack and the elbow against the other. It's useful when nothing else fits in a crack. Once you can squeeze a knee into an off-width crack, it's quite a relief.

There can be significant differences among individuals. Some people have large knees compared with their fists. You may encounter a crack in which your friend just fit a knee, but because your legs are bigger, a knee won't fit, forcing you to use a classic off-width technique.

A crack that will accommodate a knee is a real blessing. A knee jam reduces the force trying to pull you backward out of the crack, thereby increasing your options. It is achieved by flexing the knee and pulling the heel back toward your buttocks. As the muscles on the side of the knee expand, the knee fills the crack, allowing you to hang off of it, lean back, advance your upper body, chalk up, or set protection.

In classic off-width climbing, you have to deal separately with the upper and lower parts of your body. You push yourself up with your feet and hold your body in position with your arms. The feet are responsible for moving you upward, and the arms are responsible for keeping you from sliding back down or outward.

Let's say you are facing a straight-in off-width crack. You decide to take it right side in, so you stick your right leg and foot a few inches into the crack, but not so deep that you can't keep your center of gravity over your foot. Then you squeeze the right side of your upper body into the crack.

With your right arm wedged inside the crack, obtain an arm bar, palm against one side of the crack, elbow against the other side. Twist your arm toward the center of your body to gain torque. With your outside arm, grab the lip of the off-width crack and push away. You can't move up, but with the aid of those two strenuous arm movements, you can keep your body from sliding out.

With the upper body in a holding pattern:

1. Raise the right inside foot and get a heel-toe jam right inside the crack as close to beneath your weight as possible.
2. Bring the outside left foot up and get a heel-toe jam on the lip of the crack.
3. Move the left hand up slightly and grab the lip of the crack.
4. Push up with the feet and reset the right arm bar.

Following this four-beat pattern will make it easier for you to get into the flow of off-width climbing. In a long off-width crack, I often count to myself to keep my technique smooth and flowing.

An alternative technique for tackling an off-width crack is called *hand stacking*. This can usually be done only in a crack that is knee width or slightly wider. It's a method of using double jams—two hand jams, a fist jam and a hand jam, or two fist jams—and combining them in different ways. You might, for example, combine a right thumb-

Stacking a hand jam
and a fist jam.

down fist jam and a left thumb-down hand jam, wedging them both into the crack so that they are touching, not unlike wedging two stoppers together. Then, by flexing each of the jams, you can create an expansion, as you would with a single hand or fist jam.

If a hand stack is secure, you can hang from it. If, however, the stacked jams are not expanding perpendicularly against the sides of the crack, they can slide out of the crack. As with any jam, make sure it's holding before you move on it.

Next, move your legs up and support your body with a knee jam, if possible. In a wider crack, support comes from an outward-pulling heel-toe jam, with the inside leg placed in the crack high above your center of gravity and the outside leg in a heel-toe jam at the lip.

Once you set your legs and they're secure enough to hang from, you can reset your hand stack higher up the crack. In this way, you ascend, shuffling the whole way.

Elbow Lock. The elbow lock is used for wide off-widths. It's a saving move, a very efficient technique requiring almost no strength to perform.

Let's say you're in a classic off-width position, doing an arm bar. Your elbow is against one wall, your palm against the opposite wall. You rotate your forearm and flex your bicep, creating enough torque to hold yourself that way. An arm bar is strenuous and unpleasant, but you will need it when the crack is too big for a hand stack and not big enough for an elbow lock. When the crack widens enough for an elbow lock, place your palm in front of your shoulder against the far side of the crack (the side closest to your chest), while your elbow swings up and cams against the other side of the crack. It's like wedging a pipe in the crack.

The process goes like this: Hold your upper body with an elbow lock, grab the lip of the crack, then move both legs up at the same time; reset your new elbow lock and lip hold, and then shuffle up like that. It's like a classic off-width technique with the addition of the saving elbow lock, which is more secure and efficient than an arm bar.

Foot Stacking. If the crack is slightly larger, you can continue to use a secure elbow lock above. But when it gets too wide for a heel-toe jam, you must resort to foot stacking below. In foot stacking, one foot will heel-toe against the instep of the other foot.

Place the first foot in the crack, pushing the downward-pointing toes against the side; then place the instep of the second foot against the heel of the first foot. Start dropping the heel of the first foot, the toes of which are still pressed against the side of the crack. In this way, you are using the second foot as a wedge between the rock and the heel of the first foot. In effect, you are extending your foot by placing your second foot sideways, heel against arch. You can stand on a secure foot stack.

The climbing sequence goes like this: Bring the legs up, obtain a new foot stack, then slide the upper body up a foot or 6 inches, or maybe only an inch if the crack is truly horrendous. Slide a new elbow lock in, support your body with the new elbow lock and crack-rim

Foot stacking in a
wide off-width crack.

hold, bring the feet up, set a new foot stack, and slide the upper body up. It's the same wormlike movement as in a classic off-width. This combination of elbow locks and foot stacking works in thin chimneys.

Chimneys

As soon as a crack is too wide for foot stacking, you must resort to pure chimney technique.

Squeeze Chimneys. It's rare to have a crack so thin that you can't get your chest in it but wide enough to accept an elbow lock. Usually, if the elbow will fit, the chest will fit too, and you have a narrow, or squeeze, chimney.

You can climb squeeze chimneys using off-width techniques with a few added variations, one of which is a knee bar. Assuming you have a secure hold with your upper body, put your knees flush against the chest side of the crack, kind of a baby's kneeling position with the feet splayed out and the heels pressed against the other side of the crack. With both legs doing this, you can support your body weight. Moving up is difficult, however, because you don't have a lot of flexibility in this position.

The climbing sequence in a squeeze chimney goes like this: While supporting your upper body with one palm pressing downward against a wall and the other limb in an elbow lock, wiggle one hip and one knee up, set it, shift to the other side, and wiggle it up in an S-like movement. Again, it's a worm simulation, the vertical equivalent of a soldier crawling under a fence in a side-to-side squiggle.

Classic Chimneys. When cracks are so wide that they may be easily entered, you can no longer use an elbow lock or a knee bar wedge. Now you are in a classic chimney. In this size crack, you lose a certain amount of security but gain ease of climbing.

A classic chimney is less secure than a squeeze chimney, but easier to climb. Begin with one foot tucked underneath the buttocks, the other foot pressing against the far side of the crack. (*bottom*) Next, release the back foot and place it above the opposite leg so that both feet are temporarily pressing against the far wall of the crack. Then repeat the scissors position. (*top*)

In the technique for classic chimneys, one foot is against the side of the crack you are facing, the other tucked under your buttocks against the other side. Your hands are pressed against the back wall, stabilizing you, but most of the work is done by the lower body. Move the upper body up as high as you can manage comfortably, with your back leg underneath your buttocks and your front leg pushing against the wall. By pressing against the rock with, say, the left leg, you can free the right leg, placing it just above the left leg on the facing wall (both feet are temporarily on the same wall). While pressing with the right leg, put the other leg behind your buttocks and achieve a new scissors position. Stand up out of the scissors position, press your back against the wall, and reset your legs into a new scissors position.

Wide Chimneys and Inside Corners. If a crack is so wide that you can't place your back against one side of the chimney and have your foot reach the other side, it demands a stem or bridge position.

Stemming on an inside corner. The same technique can be used in a wide chimney.

Here you put a hand and a foot against each wall, each limb pressing directly out, counterpressuring against the other.

Now lean over toward the side of the foot you want to lift. Place both hands against the wall on that side, lift the foot on that side with both hands, and slide it up a few inches. Shift weight and move the hands to the other side and slide the other foot up. Keep pivoting back and forth in that manner, stemming the whole way.

Stemming is the most efficient way to climb inside corners and wide chimneys. Even if the technique is not used to make progress, it may be the best way to gain a rest; a foot thrown out to create a bridge allows your weight to rest on your legs, relieving one or both arms.

If a chimney is so wide that your feet can't reach both sides, you are left with only one possible technique, a strenuous one: You must put both feet on one side of the chimney and both hands on the other side, and simply walk up the wall, alternating hands and feet. Because your torso is absolutely horizontal, this method demands great flexibility and strength. It's like doing a handstand with someone pushing on the bottoms of your feet.

Laybacking

Some cracks may be impossible to jam. Usually it's a dihedral or a flake that offers either no jams or ones that are too technically difficult, but it could also be straight in. If that happens, you may have to resort to laybacking, which is basically what someone climbing a palm tree would do.

In laybacking, you pull with your arms while you push with your feet to create opposing pressure against opposite sides of the crack. Let's say you're laybacking in a dihedral. First grab the lip of the crack and then bring your feet up and push straight into the rock. Get those feet up pretty high but not too high. If they're too high, you put too much tension on the arms, and you won't be able to hold the position; if they're too low, however, they'll want to slip out. Find a comfortable middle position, and move one limb at a time. Don't attempt big moves during a layback. There's not a lot of searching for holds—rather, you're just shuffling up the crack.

Laybacking is straightforward, technically easy, but strenuous. It's usually very strenuous to place protection during a layback. It also may be difficult to switch from laybacking to jamming. It is an essential technique, however, one that will enable you to climb unjammable sections of rock.

Proper layback technique requires pulling with your arms and pushing with your feet—it's like climbing a palm tree.

No matter how refined your skills, there are times in climbing when you must improvise, throwing out basic technique and doing your own thing.

− 4 −

Practice

It's best to practice new techniques when you are fresh and not hindered by the fear of falling or injury. The best ways to practice are by top roping and bouldering.

Top Roping

There are three ways to top-rope a one-pitch climb. One method is to send someone to the top of the cliff, who then drops a rope down to the person who is going to do the climb. Another is to run a rope through an anchor at the top so that the climb can be protected from below (called a *yo-yo*). A third way is for the leader to lead the climb, fix an anchor at the top, and then bring the next climber up.

Top roping is a great way to develop physical, gymnastic climbing confidence. Don't be afraid to climb this way for a couple of years. Leading is fun and challenging, and you'll probably be pressured to lead by your friends. If you learn to climb while protected by a top rope, with near-zero risk of injury, you will be fully prepared to lead when the time comes. Then you will reduce the risk of falling, have less fear, and most important, enjoy it more.

When I first started, I seldom led climbs. One reason was fear. Although I could do pretty impressive boulder problems, I would freak out on the lead. I decided to perfect my technique through top-roping practice, to get so good that when I did lead, I wouldn't be bothered by it. And that's the way it happened. I was still scared, but a lot less than I would have been without the top-roping practice.

Don't succumb to peer pressure to lead before you're ready. When you do lead, stay within your limits so that you don't get hurt. In the long run, you'll get better results if you do a lengthy apprenticeship. You can master much harder moves on a top rope than you can on a scary lead.

Don't try to practice difficult moves when you're tired, lest you substitute bad technique for good. Consider the climber who decides he's going to dedicate himself to learning cracks. Imbued with an intense desire to be great, he goes out and practices cracks all day. At the end of the day, he's tired and starts to get sloppy. His concentration weakens and his hands begin to slip, causing cuts and abrasions. He is not only practicing bad technique, but injuring himself as well.

It's far better to be patient and take it slow. When learning new skills, practice only good technique. If you start to get sloppy, stop and rest or try something familiar. Go back to practicing the new skill when you're fresh and full of energy. You'll find that the quality of the time you spend is more important than quantity when it comes to learning new techniques.

Indoor Walls

Artificial climbing walls didn't exist when I started, but now they are available in many gyms. If you lack access to real rock, or if weather doesn't permit outdoor climbing, artificial walls are great. They can help you develop strength, as well as improve your technique.

You will find out, however, that indoor climbing problems are easier to read than those on real rock. Climbing on artificial walls is like climbing dot to dot. You are climbing holds that are bolted onto the wall, so it's obvious where the next hold is—it's the next blob of plastic. Real rock is more subtle, with good holds that are sometimes hidden and other holds that appear good but are worthless.

If you don't have access to a legitimate artificial wall, you can improvise. I used to go down to my local YMCA, where they had a stone wall. It wasn't built for climbing, but it had little crimper edges that I liked. I used to traverse back and forth across that; I got a great forearm workout and learned a lot about smoothing out my footwork.

Another option is to build your own artificial wall, as I did. In my backyard, I have a 36-foot overhanging climbing wall built out of plywood and 2-by-4s. It has a 4-foot starting panel at the bottom, then a gradual uphill roof section for 20 feet, followed by a 12-foot headwall at 45 degrees. Molded resin holds are bolted on. Before resin holds, I made them out of wood. I would cut them into funny shapes and sand them, and then move them around in different patterns. That allows you to try different moves on the artificial wall that should carry over to real rock.

Bouldering

Bouldering is ropeless, solo climbing usually done within jumping distance of the ground. It allows you to try moves over and over without fear of taking a life-threatening winger. Consequently, you can be relaxed, think positively, and push yourself.

When you're secured by a top rope, you can fall without consequence; when you're bouldering, however, you must be able to jump off the problem or know how to fall correctly. Most of the time, you will come off a bouldering problem in control, but not always.

In the beginning, stay away from problems where a fall might cause an injury. I teach beginners to take it step by step. I have them climb up one move, maybe a foot off the ground, and then jump off. They look at me like I'm crazy, but there's a reason for this. I then have them jump off from 2 feet, 3 feet, and before you know it they're 5 feet up, high enough that a bad landing could mean a broken wrist or a sprained ankle.

Let's say you're 5 feet up and facing a move that's giving you trouble. If you make the move, you will then be 7 feet off the ground. I suggest you go partially into the move and then take an intentional jump. You'll know that you can fall under control and that you can safely attempt the next move without worrying about landing badly and injuring yourself.

Keep jumping off the problem until you have the fall wired. You need to get the fall wired almost as much as you do the boulder problem. Fall so that your body is balanced and upright. The biggest mistake people make is landing with rigid legs. It's better to absorb the impact by going into a squat. As your feet touch the ground, sag into the landing rather than trying to resist the force, not unlike a para-chutist who squats into the landing and then rolls out of it onto his side.

One of the great things about bouldering is that you can do a lot on your own, without partners. If you are doing difficult or awkward boulder problems, you would be wise to have a spotter, but there are still ways to practice technique by yourself. Because you can practice a boulder move over and over, your technique is bound to improve.

You can do tougher moves on boulders than you can on lead. Starting fresh from the ground, you can do moves you'd never do after 50 feet of climbing. The hardest single moves in the world have all been done on boulders—and it's always going to be that way. After all, if you're obsessed with doing a boulder problem, you can conceivably try it hundreds or thousands of times over many years. Maybe you could duplicate that on lead, but it would be far more tedious, and you'd never find a partner who would put up with it.

I've had a lot of experience falling off boulder problems. There is one called "Midnight Lightning" in Camp 4 in Yosemite Valley. Before I got it, I fell about 10 feet every other day for three months. I practiced the most difficult move on "Midnight Lightning" over and over; when I finally got it, I felt like I had really learned something. I had. After that, I did the problem five to ten times a day, every other day for five years. But more than that, it gave me a new level of self-confidence that carried over to all my climbing endeavors.

Although it can be productive to go bouldering by yourself, it's usually better to go with other people, especially when you're starting out. In fact, it's the hang-loose camaraderie of bouldering that first attracted me to climbing. Growing up, I had always participated in organized sports that featured rules, uniforms, and coaches. It was somehow too cold, and I began to realize that I didn't dig it. When I first got into climbing, I'd go out to Stony Point in Southern California, and there would always be a bunch of climbers there. No uniforms, no coaches. One guy would try a problem while the rest of us would all hang around and analyze it. He'd pull a move, and if he failed and fell, you'd hear something like, "Hey, man, I saw what's missing. He pinched that hold instead of just crimping it."

It's just such tiny variables that teach you the fine art of technique. Once one person masters a move, it opens doors for others. Just three minutes earlier, when everybody was failing, you would have heard,

"This is impossible, man, nobody could do this." Breakthroughs are common in bouldering, especially with other people around to help out.

One guy who did it alone was John Gill, probably the greatest boulderer who ever lived. Thirty years ago, he solved boulder problems by himself that the best boulderers in the world haven't been able to repeat to this day. He probably would have appreciated others pushing him, but there was no one around who could even touch him.

Bouldering success can provide the confidence you need to succeed high up on a rock face. I was doing 5.10 and 5.11 boulder problems long before I was able to do that on lead. Why? Mostly for psychological reasons—the same reasons why you can walk a tightwire 2 feet off the ground but are thrown into a tizzy when it's 500 feet up. Concentration is a lot harder with so much at risk. If you fall from a boulder, people might laugh at you; if you fall on the lead, you may get seriously injured or even killed.

It's just so easy to walk up to a boulder problem, work at it for two hours, trying it forty times. You can attack the most horrendous moves over and over on a boulder. Even hangdogging from a top rope isn't as good a study as sitting at the foot of a boulder problem.

If you can do all the boulder problems in your area, it will give you a huge psychological boost when you're leading. That's what happened to me. I would face something challenging and think, "This move is so easy compared with some of the boulder problems I've done. So how come I'm scared up here?" Finally, in part because of the confidence I'd developed through my success in doing boulder problems, I made a critical psychological leap. I came to realize that there was no reason to be afraid. Once I convinced myself that the moves were easy, I knew—really knew—that I wasn't going to fall. Although I still had respect for falling, my attitude was that it was not going to happen.

A lot of people skip bouldering, but that's a mistake. It really is the best way to develop the confidence needed to carry you up the rock.

Static and Dynamic Moves

The two main ways of moving on the rock are *static* and *dynamic*. In the beginning, keep in mind the three-point rule: Maintain three points of contact with the rock, and move only the fourth point, either a hand or a foot. This is static climbing.

Static refers to the ability of the climber to hold in a certain position while he touches a new hold, grabs it, tests it, adjusts his hand, and if he doesn't like the new hold, finds a different one. Static climbing looks very deliberate: The body freezes, a limb moves to a new hold, the body shifts to a new four-point position, one limb moves to another hold, the body moves, locks off, reaches with the fourth limb, and so on. It's a way of breaking down a climb into individual pieces.

Three-point static climbing is a valuable tactic in scary situations because it enables you to downclimb. Let's say you get up ten moves and have had enough. If you've developed the ability to remember the individual moves, you can reverse each one and undo anything you've done.

This is much more difficult, if not impossible, with dynamic moves, in which you have fewer than three points of contact with the rock. Let's say you can't hold a lock-off position and reach up and feel for the next hold. Maybe your present hold is so bad that you can only hold on for a short time. You look a couple of feet above you and see a great hold, a bucket. So you decide to use momentum to launch yourself and grab that hold. This is an all-or-nothing move. If you miss, you fall.

Dynos, as they're called, may also be used when you have a solid hold and a long reach. Let's say you have a great hold, with another good one 4 feet above and nothing in between. The only way to reach it is with a giant lunge. The best time to throw the hand up and grab the hold is at the peak of the lunge, at the change of direction, also called the *deadpoint*. At that moment of zero velocity, just before gravity starts to drag you back down, make the grab.

A great place to practice dynamos is on boulders. You can try your lunge a million times. And if you get into bouldering, you'll discover that some of the greatest problems in the world are lunges, like some of the ones John Gill did. He was a dynamo master. He did a double dynamo on "Fatted Calf" in Pueblo, Colorado, and thirty years later it has still not been repeated. With a double dynamo, you start from a dead hang, lunge upward, and all four limbs leave the rock. Your body is airborne in an upward flight path, and at the top of the flight path, just before you start dropping, you grab the new hold. It's a spectacular, scary technique that's rarely used except on boulder problems.

Often the deciding factor with a dynamo is the risk assessment. You may conclude that you have nothing to lose. For example, if you have to decide between a 30-foot fall and a dynamo, falling obviously gives you a 0 percent chance of making it, while the dynamo may give you a 10 percent chance.

Tempo

How fast should you climb? Let's say you have a steep face climb, and it looks like your arms are going to get pumped. Should you climb fast and get through it quickly? One school of thought holds that the less time you spend climbing a tough section, the less time you hang on your arms and the less energy you use. That's probably true if it's a straightforward climb with similar moves, like a brick wall. But on a climb that demands thinking about each move, you must find a balance between fast and slow. If you go fast, you may rely on such mechanically disadvantageous technique that it drains energy more quickly.

Everyone's point of balance is different. I like to climb slower than some people. Because I save so much energy using smooth technique, it's more efficient for me. You'll have to experiment. Be aware of the two extremes and find your point somewhere in between. Move slowly enough to maintain smooth technique; it's more efficient, and you won't reinforce bad habits for future routes.

My tempo is different when I'm free-soloing. Roped, I'm not so preoccupied with precise positioning, and I might put my foot in a less-than-ideal position, but free-soloing I take more time and place my feet perfectly. In both cases, I try to relax the parts of my body I'm not using.

Mental Practice

> "You can't think and hit at the same time."
>
> —Yogi Berra

Climbing is every bit as much a mental exercise as it is a physical one. You must repeatedly convince yourself that you are doing well. It's a conviction that will enable you to stay relaxed, which is so critical. Just what are the obstacles to being relaxed?

Let's say you have good balance and can stand on a tightwire strung a foot off the ground. But if you walk to the edge of a cliff, you can't get close enough to look down. Why not? It's because your mind is dwelling on other matters, like falling. And all that mental interference is obstructing your ability to concentrate. Irrational thoughts intrude: "What if I have a sudden twitch? What if a wind comes up?" None of that is going to happen, of course, but your mind has become your enemy; most of your attention and energy are draining into areas that can't do you any good. Such thinking causes a lot of tension to build up in your muscles, inhibiting athletic performance. Instead, you should be focused on the task at hand.

Another common example is the climber who can do easy moves on a crag 2 feet off the ground a thousand times in a row. He never makes a mistake. But as soon as he gets 20 feet above his protection, he freezes up and can't do the move. It's the same physical event, but it tweaks him mentally to be facing that long a fall.

A trick I use is to completely convince myself that the only way for me to survive what I'm doing is to concentrate. I work myself into what is almost a crazed state of mind, where I block out everything else, where I see only what I'm doing. By visualizing perfect movement, by seeing myself floating up the rock, I minimize the possibility of anything negative happening. This is, however, after I've checked my protection and looked honestly at my situation. "I can take a fall here," I might conclude. "It's a safe fall, and there's no way I'll get hurt. So don't worry about falling. I'm master of stone and have no chance of falling."

Besides visualizing general success, it's important to break down the climb into individual moves. Before I start, I stand at the bottom and scrutinize the route, previsualizing, plotting out how I'm going to grab a certain edge, where I'm going to put my foot when the crack narrows, what moves will and won't work. I will try to identify the crux of the climb and presolve it, if possible. If the moves don't seem obvious, I may even make up two or three possible solutions to the crux.

For strength moves, I practice mental imagery. I might pretend that a light switch has suddenly been turned on, that electricity is surging through me, and that there's nothing anybody can do to stop it. This works great for a pure power move. On the other hand, when I have to do a one-arm hang from an edge for several seconds, I imagine that my fingers are steel hooks. It helps to have a vivid imagination. Believing is power.

Another way I neutralize fear is to run a circular mantra through my mind: "Relax, breathe, concentrate . . . relax, breathe, concentrate . . ." I don't actually say it but think it. It is the perfect antidote for the accumulation of tension. After all, you have to be relaxed to perform your best in any sport. Note that you are not turning off your mind or the muscles that are tensed during that one-arm lock-off, but you are relaxing the muscles not in use.

If I find myself getting tense, I know I'm not breathing properly. In response, I try to focus on the fluid, rhythmic flow of my breathing. As soon as I start breaking that pattern, my concentration deteriorates, and I start to substitute sloppy movement for good clean moves, something I detest in myself. I seek to move smoothly on the rock, which is as important as making the climb. That's a big reason I free-solo. Maybe I'm not doing the hardest routes solo—and of course, you can't—but soloing is a great way to develop an efficient, clean style. I'm like a dancer who gets satisfaction feeling the relative ease of perfect movement. When I start to struggle and can't think straight, which most people can't when they are gripped, I return to "Relax, breathe, concentrate . . ." It works well for me; maybe it will for you, too.

Intellectually, I have to make all possible outcomes favorable. If there's a chance I will fall on, say, the fifth move, will it be a safe fall? If it's a possible bad fall, I probably won't go for it. And if I do go for it, I will climb more statically, less dynamically.

Of course, risk assessment is very much a function of how serious a fall you face. How much go-for-it you have should depend in part on the chances of damaging your body. If there's absolutely no chance of getting hurt, you can just do the move without distraction. Five feet off the ground with a soft, flat landing, you can try any move in the world. You could fall on your back and be okay. At 10 feet you start to hesitate; if you fall on your back now, you could get hurt. At 15 feet you could sprain an ankle. At 20 feet you could crack an ankle—and your head. At 30 feet you could do some real damage. If you fall from 50 feet, you'll live only if you're lucky.

As things get tougher, as the risk builds, you should be slowing down, previsualizing more. Everyone is different, but I tend to become more conservative, doing more static moves and fewer dynamic ones, making sure that any move I do is reversible. Someone else might reason, "Ah, there's only a 10 percent chance that I'll break both ankles—I'll go for the glory!" But I've been injured enough that I don't think that way. If you climb long enough, the percentages will eventually catch up with you. Instead, I recall the old saying "He who climbs and runs away lives to climb another day."

Free Soloing

Free soloing is the art of moving up the rock without the aid of equipment, ropes, or partners. It's definitely not for everyone, and certainly not for beginners. If you decide to try it, make sure you know what you're getting into. Talk with people who've tried it already, and take it slow.

When asked, I say that I started free-soloing when I was sixteen, but it really depends on your definition of the term. People free-solo every day just walking to the store; the real issue is the difficulty of the route. I didn't consider what I did free soloing until I soloed a route that ordinarily called for a rope. Sure, I could solo 5.5, but that's easy; a lot of people can do 5.5. Back when I started, no one really soloed anything above 5.8—it was just considered stupid.

In the Yosemite Decimal System, routes are classified as follows:

Class 1: A walk.

Class 2: A hike or easy scramble; proper footwear required.

Class 3: Ropes sometimes advised, not because the climb is so difficult, but because a fall could be injurious or fatal.

Class 4: Most climbers—except free soloists—use ropes.

Class 5.0 to 5.14: The heart of the matter for free climbers. Ropes required, except by free soloists. The most difficult climbs are further subdivided into a, b, c, and d.

Class 6: Aid climbing.

One day when I was sixteen, I went climbing with John Long. He said we were going to do a 5.8 route at Joshua Tree, called "Double Cross." I said okay, let's go do it. We were walking toward the climb when I said, "Hey, the car's over there. We have to get the ropes."

"We're not using ropes," he said. "We're going to solo it."

"Well, I'm not. I can't do that," I said.

"Look at it this way," he said, sounding very reasonable. "If you did the route a hundred times, how many times would you fall?"

I thought about it, but only for a moment. "Well . . . never. I'd never fall. It's not possible."

"So that's it, then. We're soloing it."

I had to admit, albeit reluctantly, that John made sense. Emboldened by his logic, I soloed "Double Cross," and I've never used a rope on it since.

Bachar's five tips for free soloists:

1. If you quit free-soloing now, you greatly reduce serious risks to your health.

2. He who downclimbs and runs away lives to free-solo another day. Climb one move at a time, and always be prepared to reverse if the next move seems too hard.

3. Never bite off more than you can chew; always climb solo well beneath your roped free-climbing capabilities.

4. You can fool your friends into thinking you're in control; never fool yourself. If you feel scared, the route is too hard for you to solo.

5. Style and control are the hallmarks of a great free soloist. No summit, however prestigious or desirable, is worth the sacrifice of these qualities.

As with any other type of climbing, there is risk involved. Storms, rock falls, and breaking holds are just a few of the uncontrollable hazards that can occur when you're high on the rock without a way to get down quickly or move safely. When free-soloing you should start low and work up slowly. Become comfortable with one level before you attempt something harder. When I first started, I thought, "Boy, wouldn't it be great to solo 5.11?" Then, when I was nineteen, I soloed a 5.11—Yosemite's 400-foot "New Dimensions"—and 5.11 became easy. Soon I was climbing routes that had seemed ridiculously hard a short while before.

When I soloed "New Dimensions," I didn't tell anybody. Word

somehow spread through the climber's camp, but nobody would talk to me about it. I could hear them whispering behind my back, "There goes John Bachar. He soloed 'New Dimensions.'" Nobody understood it. Somebody posted a message on the camp bulletin board: "Tell Webster's to change the meaning of insanity to `John Bachar free-soloing New Dimensions'!"

But it wasn't insanity, at least for me. It was simply a matter of stretching what I thought was possible. When I first soloed a 5.12—"Leave it to Beaver" in Joshua Tree—it was one of the first 5.12s in the world to be soloed. Now I solo 5.12 every other day.

The main objective of free soloing is, in my opinion, to feel a sense of control on the rock. I try to achieve—even if I'm the only one around—beautiful, smooth, efficient technique. The goal is far more than just reaching the top. I've made it to the top of a lot of climbs that scared me. And when you scare yourself free-soloing, it doesn't feel good. In fact, you feel nauseous and terrible for hours, maybe days. It's a huge, possibly irrevocable, setback. It's better to back off and tackle something a notch less difficult, a route you can dominate, than it is to stretch yourself too far.

If you stay with climbing and try to improve, you will inevitably stretch your limits. After all, the first time you solo a 5.7 after doing 5.6s, it's a stretch. But the advance should not be made until you have dominated the previous level of rope climbing. You will feel when it's right.

Another important lesson that's especially applicable to free soloing is that you can fool others with a cool facade, but don't try to fool yourself. Free soloing is life or death. You may look cool to those watching from below, but deep inside you know if you didn't feel secure on a move. And one bad move is all it takes to kill yourself.

People can't stand to watch a free soloist who's out of control. They turn away. The attitude is that if he's going to fall and die, they don't want to see it. Some people can't stand to watch even a good free soloist—it just looks too dangerous.

But soloists don't fall very often; they can't afford to. I've taken only one serious fall. On a difficult solo in Colorado's Eldorado Springs Canyon, I tumbled 20 feet. My balance allowed me to land right side up, but then a dislodged rock knocked me down, badly bruising my back. After standing up, I fainted. When I came to, I drove myself home.

My buddy Rick Cashner has twice fallen more than 30 feet. The average climber will die from a fall of more than 47 feet, but 30 feet can do a lot of damage. Rick's a tough guy. He's broken a few bones, lost a few teeth, but he's still a climber. That's the way it is—real climbers do it for life. The first time Rick fell, he knocked out his front teeth and gashed his eyebrow pretty bad. A ranger scrambled up to him and found blood spurting from Rick's brow. He thought it was coming from his eye and fainted, hitting his head on a rock and knocking himself out. Rick hiked out to get help for the ranger. Like I said, he's a tough guy.

I'm often asked whether, as a free soloist, I worry about leading unsuspecting novices to their death. I used to battle this issue with Yosemite's former chief ranger, Bill Wendt, who once halted a television shoot of me in the park until assurances were given that the program would carry a safety message. "It's too easy to copy someone on TV," he said. "Anyone attempting to free-solo should realize that Bachar is at an Olympic level."

I disagree with Wendt about the likelihood of novices copying accomplished free soloists. The sport has a built-in safety device. Someone who doesn't know what he's doing isn't going to get very far up a 5.11 climb. The beginner will drop out long before Zone 3 (which means if you fall, you die). The numbers back this up: Of the approximately 850 mountaineering and rock-climbing fatalities in the United States from 1951 to 1984, only one was the result of a free-solo rock-climbing fall.

Whether you climb with or without a rope, you have to be sensible and careful. Without those qualities, you should stay home. Of course, it also helps to be extremely lucky. Consider the climber who was doing "Reed's Direct," a 5.9 climb in Yosemite. Not only was he tied in, but he also had a drag line for hauling up equipment. Most people don't even have a drag line on that climb. He fell from 150 feet up, but he had tied in to his harness wrong, and the rope ripped apart the harness. He would have been history, except that his drag line wrapped around a tree on the wall, caught, and stopped him 5 feet from the ground. It made quite an impression on him. After that, he sold all his equipment and quit climbing.

Fear

First, let me clarify a misconception: I don't think I know anyone who isn't afraid of heights. I've been terrified of heights ever since I can remember. But practice reduces fear to a manageable level, a level that forces me to concentrate. I zoom right in. It's a relaxed sort of concentration. I get so focused on doing each movement with grace and control that it makes no difference whether I'm 50 feet up or 5.

I control fear by intellectually convincing myself that everything is okay. I tell myself that my anchors are absolutely bombproof or, if I'm soloing, that each move is secure, that I've done harder moves before. It's the same sort of confidence I have walking down the street knowing I'm not going to fall over.

Once you develop that confidence, height is no big deal. People always ask if I look down. Of course, I look down; it's beautiful up there. If you achieve the mental state I'm describing, it's no more terrifying looking down from 1,000 feet than from 6 inches. Just looking down isn't going to kill you; it's the possibility of falling that makes you afraid. I counter that possibility by double-checking my anchors or focusing on my technique. There is, after all, no logical reason to feel that you're going to fall; experience teaches the veteran that the harness and rope aren't going to shred, the jam isn't going to slip. When you truly accept that, height becomes enjoyable.

Some people are obsessed with the dangers of climbing—especially soloing—but what they don't realize is that just about every move is reversible. If it's too hard, I can undo it. That's not the case with, say, speed skiing or hang gliding. In those sports, once you've started, you're committed.

– 5 –

Training

No matter how advanced your free-climbing techniques, you'll still need a certain amount of strength to perform most of the moves. Some techniques permit more mechanical advantages than others, and hence demand less strength. Elbow locks and heel-toes, for example, require almost no strength. But they are the exceptions. Training increases your capacity for strength, power, and injury prevention. If you find yourself facing a big fall, straining so hard to hang on that you pull a muscle or a finger tendon, you will understand the importance of training.

The specific exercises you choose to emphasize in your training program should depend on your strengths and weaknesses and the type of climbing—crack or face—that you favor, but the principles remain the same. Try to train for power rather than for endurance. Climbing is mostly anaerobic—that is, it's exercise at an intensity level that recruits mostly fast-twitch muscle groups that function without oxygen. Consequently, it can only be sustained for a short while before muscular failure results. Even a generous hold on which a trained climber might hang for two minutes is a fifty-fifty split between aerobic and anaerobic muscle groups.

The anaerobic muscles are the power muscles that work without oxygen. They are the ones that enable you to do a 100-yard dash or a one-arm pull-up. They derive their energy from the glycogen stored right in the muscle, which is burned quickly. The reason you can't run a marathon at a 100-yard-dash pace is that those muscles begin to fail rapidly.

I advocate weight training and resistance exercises tailored for climbing movements. Power training demands higher resistance and fewer repetitions of movement. (To improve pure endurance, apply less resistance and more reps.) An organized exercise program is a good, safe way to increase strength, reduce injuries, and build confidence. It's good for your body, even if you're not a serious climber. You can try to increase strength on the rock merely by hanging on to holds a little longer, but that's not very scientific—or effective. You cannot precisely control the amount of resistance applied to the muscles. On the other hand, doing weight training and resistance exercises in a gym allows you to control all the variables—speed of movement, amount of resistance, duration—in a logical, safe manner that promotes growth.

There are two types of muscular contractions in climbing: *isometric* and *isotonic*. Lots of climbing muscles work isotonically—that is, with movement. They are forever pulling in or letting out under tension, as in pull-ups. Others work isometrically. When you stand for a minute in a toe hold or grab an edge and hold on without changing the position of your fingers, the critical muscles are working under static tension, or isometrically.

If you are training for isometric moves, you should emphasize isometric exercises; isotonic moves, on the other hand, demand isotonic exercises. There is a little crossover between the two, but not much.

Becoming a complete climber means training both isometrically and isotonically. Fingers are always trained isometrically, for example by hanging for specific intervals on doorjambs or hanging boards. If you're going to be facing strenuous pull-ups on steep overhangs, then you have to train for the isotonic action of your arm pulling up and in toward your body. Some climbing moves—and most climbs—require both. You may have to pull up isotonically and then lock off isometrically, using the same muscle groups.

A good exercise with which to begin is the old standard: two-arm pull-ups on a horizontal bar. After all, climbing is a pulling sport. Start by determining how many pull-ups you can do. One person may be able to do five, another twenty. It doesn't matter; you simply need to establish your starting point.

The difference between someone who can do five and someone

who can do twenty may be that the latter has more anaerobic (fast-twitch) muscle fibers. This is genetic to a certain extent, but training can make a big difference. As a sophomore in high school, I was next to last in the pull-up contest. I beat only the class bookworm. I did two; he did one. Meanwhile, others in my class were banging out twenty-five or thirty.

So at fourteen, my starting point was two pull-ups. But I liked climbing and wanted to do more of it, so I stayed with the pull-ups. And one day, I was able to do three . . . then four . . . then five. A year later, I could do ten, which was about average at my high school. I began doing sets of ten pull-ups, as many as ten sets a day. I just kept increasing the numbers, and by the time I was a senior, I could do twenty-seven pull-ups. In two years I had moved from two to twenty-seven. I knew the tricks, such as using a circular pull-up motion so that the body is moving toward the bar as the chin reaches it, but I was also a lot stronger. I thought I was hot stuff. But actually, I was very limited. All I ever did was pull-ups and parallel-bar dips.

When I was twenty-two, I began reading kinesiology books; they taught me that I was doing it all wrong. Power lifters have long known the right way to train, but it hadn't filtered down to climbers. The Russians, who have won countless power-lifting competitions, have studied this intently. They adhere to the SAID principle—specific adaptation to imposed demands—which means that your body will adapt to the demands imposed on it. For example, if you walk around barefoot, you eventually get calluses on your feet; if you grab a lot of small holds, you get calluses on your fingertips.

Reading on, I learned that if you haul big rocks around, something you can do for only a few seconds, you become powerful. Just as you do when you latch on to small holds that you can grip for only five seconds before your muscles turn to butter. Both are power moves using anaerobic muscle fibers, which burn fuel quickly (as opposed to aerobic fibers, which use oxygen and continuously make fuel).

Studying kinesiology taught me that what's important is not how many pull-ups you can do, but how much resistance you can handle doing just one pull-up. After all, climbing isn't a sport that forces you to yank off thirty straight pull-ups; it's a sport that demands the big power move to get you over a lip. A lot of people think that if they can do thirty pull-ups, they'll be great climbers. But it's not necessarily so. The key is quality, not quantity. John Gill, the great boulderer, knew that. He regularly did one-arms with weights, probably because of his gymnastic background.

Needing to increase my power, I started doing pull-ups with a weight belt strapped around my waist. I rather quickly reached the point where I could do a clean two-arm pull-up with 140 pounds. And suddenly I could do a one-arm pull-up. From age fourteen to age twenty-two, I had increased my pull-ups from two to maybe thirty, but I still couldn't do a one-arm pull-up. I started adding weight, and by the time I was in my late twenties, I could do a one-arm pull-up (left arm) with 12½ pounds (the world record is about 57 pounds from a dead hang) and a two-arm pull-up (shoulders to the bar) with 140 pounds.

The key was increasing power. I got better results in a short time by adding weight than I did doing one hundred pull-ups a day for eight years. In all, I've trained every other day for twenty years. Some would say that's a lot, but if I'd started adding weight in my teens, I might have been able to do two-arm pull-ups with 160 pounds.

The *Guinness Book of World Records* says that one person in a hundred thousand can do a one-arm pull-up. Clearly, it's not for everybody, no matter how much they train. One day I was working out at a Gold's Gym. Nearby was a man named Ken Waller, who had recently been national bodybuilding champion. He was whipping off bench presses with 150-pound dumbbells in each hand. It occurred to me that he could have squashed me with his pinkie.

He saw me doing one-arms and came over to try. But he couldn't get off the ground. I suggested he pull up with two arms and then let go of one. He dropped like a stone. Because he had not specifically trained for one-arm pull-ups, his great strength gave him no advantage. Of course, if he had been training to do one-arm pull-ups instead of bench presses, he probably could have done one with me in his other hand.

Workout Plan

In devising a workout plan, the key is to seek improvements incrementally. No matter how much desire you have, you can't go from couch potato to callused feet by hiking 20 miles barefoot. It doesn't happen in one day. On the other hand, if you never walk barefoot, you will never get any response at all.

Another catchy acronym is GAS: general adaptation syndrome. This is the idea that your body generally adapts to new stresses placed on it. If you have to carry buckets of water from the river to your camp every day, your shoulders and legs are going to get stronger.

Let's say that like a fourteen-year-old John Bachar, you can do two pull-ups. Begin then by doing sets of two. Do lots of sets. Try hard, but not so hard that you're straining. You don't want to risk rupturing a tendon or pulling a muscle. Keep your form. If you feel your form changing—your shoulders start curling up toward your ear, your elbows start flying out—take it as a sign to quit.

Eventually, build up to three pull-ups. Then five . . . then ten. One day, you reach the point where you can comfortably do three sets of ten without straining. Now it's time to add some weight to a weight belt—maybe 2 pounds—and see if you can do a pull-up.

Then try one pull-up with 5 pounds. If that works, try one pull-up with 10 pounds. If you can do it, but only by straining, go back to 5 pounds. See how many you can do with 5 pounds without straining. Try to do five or six. Maybe you feel like you could do seven or eight, but stop if you feel the strain and instead do a couple of sets of five. Slowly build up more weight.

If you can do three sets of ten pull-ups, you might pick a weight that allows you to do eight without straining. So maybe your daily workout becomes three sets of eight and one set of five, with weights. That's only twenty-nine pull-ups a day. It doesn't seem like much, but they are quality pull-ups. And there's an inverse relationship between quality and quantity. When you add weight, you necessarily reduce the number of pull-ups. Instead of one hundred a day, you may do fifty, or thirty. You may not feel as pumped, but your tendons are receiving more stress. And you are building more power.

Going out climbing and grabbing tiny holds will have an undeniable training effect, but you can control it better in a gym. It's also safer. There are plenty of climbers who decided to train by climbing one-finger pockets, only to blow out a finger tendon, shelving them for the next nine months. Intelligent training in the gym significantly reduces your chance of injury.

Doing one pull-up with weight will stress tendons—and produce a growth response—better than the thirtieth unweighted pull-up of a set.

Isometric Exercises

The basic isometric exercise that is essential for climbers is the finger-tip hang. Grab a nice first-knuckle, $3/4$-inch edge and see how long you can hang on it. Maybe you can hang five seconds, maybe ten, maybe sixty. In any event, the principles are the same as they were for the isotonic exercises: start low and increase gradually.

Or say you find a larger edge, one you can hang on for twenty seconds. Try three to six hangs for fifteen to twenty seconds each. This should require effort without straining. That is, it should be the kind of edge on which you fail at about twenty-two seconds.

I like to pick an edge on which I can hang for eleven or twelve seconds and do three ten-second hangs. Then maybe I do three twenty-second hangs on a larger edge and three thirty-second hangs on a still larger edge. In the beginning, total hang time should not exceed more than three minutes.

When you improve sufficiently—let's say you can now hang on a first-knuckle edge for a minute or so—it's time to add weights. Start out by adding 10 pounds and see what you can do. You will have to gauge for yourself how much weight you can start with, but try to improve to smaller edges and more weight.

I can hang on a good first-knuckle edge for fifteen seconds with 130 pounds around my waist, so I might do three to five hangs for five seconds with 125 pounds, then three ten-second hangs with 100 pounds, followed by three twenty-second hangs with 75 pounds and three thirty-second hangs with 50 pounds. I balance it so that the total hang time is about five minutes. The more powerful the moves, the more resting I do—at least two or three minutes—in between sets of hangs.

One caveat: It's dangerous to add so much weight that you fail at isometrics in less than five seconds or isotonics in fewer than five repetitions. If I can do only two pull-ups with 130 pounds, training at such a high level of resistance is unsafe. Years later, you might do few repetitions and short hang times, but that's way down the road when you know more.

I'm often asked how to start doing one-arm pull-ups. Actually, there are several possibilities. You can reduce resistance by attaching elastic bands to the pull-up bar and putting your other arm or foot in them. You can use a lat pulldown machine. You can try holding a static one-arm at the $1/4$, $1/2$, and $3/4$ position to gain strength. You can try holding at the lock-off position, with the shoulders even with the bar. You can use the other hand as a helper, holding the stressed arm, then easing off and trying to maintain the position.

When I started in this sport, about the only exercises climbers did were pull-ups and fingertip pull-ups, and whether those even helped was hotly debated. Now it's a known fact: They help, and so do others. There are plenty of exercises you should be doing just for basic joint and tendon health; consult some weight-training books for details on that subject.

If you are at least a semiserious climber, include exercises that counter all the pulling you do in training and climbing. Do some pressing—push-ups, for example. Work out the antagonistic muscle groups that are neglected in climbing, seeking a general muscular balance. If you develop certain muscles and not their opposites, you end up with irregularities and imbalances in your muscle tension, which unduly stresses joints.

Typically, climbers are much better pullers than pushers. With their well-developed lats, they have strong upper backs but relatively weak fronts. They have strong biceps but weak triceps. Maybe they can do one hundred pull-ups but can't do many push-ups or dips. A climber with such imbalances is vulnerable to dislocated shoulders, among other injuries. The shoulder, held in place by a variety of muscle groups, will have a tendency to slip out in the direction of strength.

Flexibility

Besides strength, climbers need flexibility to be effective. They achieve this through stretching. There are back stretches, finger stretches, arm and leg stretches.

I believe it's a mistake to stretch when you're cold, as a warm-up, which is exactly what a lot of people do. It's better to begin with, say, a twenty-minute walk to elevate the body temperature, the muscle temperature, so that tissues are more pliable. Another common mistake is to stretch too far too fast, what is called *ballistic stretching*.

Try to stretch a few times a day while you're warmed up. Buy a book or take a yoga class to learn specific stretching exercises. Concentrate especially on the legs, a weak point for many climbers. If hamstring and groin muscles are too tight, you will have trouble lifting your legs high enough to take advantage of all the footholds. Flexibility will allow you to use more of the natural features on the rock and will boost your confidence as a climber.

Scheduling

According to the GAS principle, when you first apply stress, the body weakens. If you walk around barefoot, your feet get sore. The next day, you wear shoes; the third day, your feet are a little tougher. If you go bouldering and tear the skin on your fingers, a couple of days later, your skin is tougher. You have experienced growth, adaptation.

Rest is a key ingredient in this equation. When you apply stress, you have to give the body a chance to recover. Rest days are every bit as important as workout days; it is during rest that the real growth takes place.

For me, climbing and working out every other day is best. I'll climb Monday morning and train Monday afternoon, and on Tuesday I won't climb at all. I might take a hike or jog, but nothing longer than a half hour, nothing strenuous, and nothing requiring hands. Wednesday is another climbing and workout day.

Weekend climbers might take a slightly different approach. A good schedule for weekenders would be to train on Tuesday and Thursday and climb on Saturday and Sunday. If you adopt that strategy, however, beware of one pitfall. If you've climbed well on Saturday, feeling strong and fresh, you may try to repeat the experience on Sunday only to be frustrated when you can't duplicate Saturday's effort. It's best to take it easier the second day. Work on technique, have fun, but don't expect the same strength and energy you demonstrated on Saturday. The fact is, if you climb two days in a row, you're going to be stronger on one of those days, usually the first. You may pull off the route you attempt on day two, but you'll be operating with slightly fatigued muscles, and with a greater risk of injury.

Injuries

Prevention. Injuries are a real downer: We don't think about them much until they happen, then we may be down for months.

The first and best way to prevent injuries is to schedule your activities wisely. I mentioned the need for rest days; let's take it a step further. Let's say you climb and train hard on Monday and then make Tuesday a rest day. By Wednesday, you still haven't completely recuperated. Since you can't hit it hard like you did on Monday, Wednesday becomes a medium day. You might do routes of three-quarters difficulty, then weight training at one-half your maximum. Thursday is another rest day. Friday you should be feeling strong again and can return to nearly what you did on Monday.

In any given week, you're going to have one day when you feel your best. It seems that every five to seven days you have a day you can't repeat for five to seven days. You're so powered, so full of energy that you think it will carry over to the next day. But your body has cycles, and unfortunately it doesn't operate at such an elevated state very often.

We can find guidance in the top-flight power-lifting programs. The schedule looks like this:

Monday: heavy day
Tuesday: rest day
Wednesday: light day
Thursday: rest day
Friday: medium day with low resistance
Saturday: rest day
Sunday: rest day
Monday: another heavy day

World-class power lifters really have only one heavy day a week. They recognize that recuperation is just as important, just as necessary, as the application of stress. If you apply stress and don't recuperate, you're not going to get stronger.

Treatment and Rehabilitation. There are two main types of injuries: *traumatic* and *overuse*. Let's say you tackle a hard route. You reach a one-finger pocket, and when you try to pull on it, you feel a pop in the finger tendon. Or maybe you find yourself in an awkward layback, with your shoulders above your head, when suddenly you feel a twinge in your shoulder. These are traumatic injuries, as are falling and breaking a wrist or ankle and dislocating a shoulder. Overuse injuries—most commonly elbows, finger tendons, and rotator cuff shoulders—are usually caused by doing too much too fast with too little rest.

In both traumatic and overuse injuries, treatment is the same. Immediately rest the injured part. You can use ice at first to control the inflammation. But after three to five days, I believe that you should start to rehabilitate the injured muscle or tendon. That may be a long or short process, depending on the severity of the injury, but it's a necessary one. If the injury is severe or new to you, or if there is constant pain, see a doctor, preferably a specialist who is well versed in sports medicine.

The rehabilitation principle is the same as the training principle: You have to apply enough stress to produce a growth response but not so much as to produce a destructive response. If you apply too much stress to a tendon or muscle, healthy or not, you will produce a debilitated body part that cannot recuperate. And that's what an injury is. Whether it improves in fourteen days or fourteen months depends on how far you've crossed over the stress line.

Say you're climbing and feel a little pop in a tendon. It doesn't hurt much then or right after the climb. It's a little tight, a little achy, but the symptoms are vague. So you rest the next day, then go climbing. Again you feel discomfort. If it's tendinitis, the classic overuse injury, you will feel a twinge of pain just as you are releasing from a hold. That's because you feel the pain most acutely when the greatest stress is applied, and the greatest stress is applied during the negative, or eccentric, part of the flexation.

There are two phases of an isotonic exercise: concentric, in which the movement of the limb makes the muscle get shorter, as in a pull-up; eccentric, or negative, in which the limb's movement makes the muscle gets longer, as in the downward movement after a pull-up. Weight-training coaches discourage negatives. The destructive nature of negatives is deceptive, because it seems easier to let yourself down from a pull-up than to do the actual pull-up. But in actuality you're applying more stress. Some argue that it's that part of the pull-up that causes the strength response. There's no question that it's the part that causes the injury response.

You can't avoid the coming down, but you can minimize it—at

least in the gym. Try using a chair when you do pull-ups. That will shorten, though not eliminate, the downward journey. At the top, just after that micropause between the concentric and eccentric movements, you will still experience the sudden jolt of added stress. And if you feel pain or high-level discomfort, you probably have tendinitis.

Regardless of the type of injury, if you feel pain, you need to decrease your activity level to the point where you feel no pain. Doctors used to tell injured climbers not to do anything for nine months; now they recommend exercising lightly, staying below the pain threshold.

Rehabilitation can be a long, winding, up-and-down road. You are forced to detour, backtrack. I can normally do side dumbbell lifts with 50 or 60 pounds, but I started rehabilitation of an injured shoulder tendon lifting 1-pound weights. Even that hurt, though only a little. But the movement increased circulation, which accelerated the removal of dead cells from the area. A lot of achiness is due to the stagnation of blood in an injured part of the body.

I personally don't believe in fighting these problems with anti-inflammatory drugs. First, I think inflammation serves a beneficial purpose. Second, dealing with a partially ruptured tendon by attacking the inflammation is treating the symptoms, not the cause of the injury.

I also disagree with a lot of so-called experts about treating tendinitis with ice. I might use ice for the first couple of days after the injury, but then I rely on heat and mild exercises to increase circulation and rehabilitate the area. Heat speeds up chemical reactions needed to heal the injured area; ice slows them down and prolongs the injury.

There are plenty of exercises for an injured body part. Last year I hurt the pronator in my elbow—the muscle that allows us to turn the palm inward toward the center of the body. I hurt it because after twenty-two years of climbing, my forearms and biceps are very strong, while the back of my forearms and triceps are relatively weak. This caused my joint to shift and put a lot of stress on my pronator. I had a terrible time with that muscle because I had never done exercises to strengthen the auxiliary muscles of the elbow, like the pronator and the supinator. Now I do them all the time. There's nothing like an injury to motivate you—and to reveal your weaknesses.

To help prevent injury, incorporate rehab exercises into your training program even before you become injured, because as you build up certain muscles used in climbing, your auxiliary muscles will become relatively weaker, making you prone to injury in those areas. Unfortunately, most people don't learn this lesson until they are already injured.

Restarting. When you're coming back from an injury and are well enough to get back on the rock, it's good to start out with routes you know well. If you're already familiar with every move, you will likely avoid awkward positions that would aggravate your injury.

If you damage tendon or muscle tissue and don't stress it with exercise while it's healing, it repairs itself in a clumpy, irregular pattern, like a scab. On the other hand, applying stress to the healing tissue through rehab exercises causes it to re-form in a more regular—and hence stronger—line.

When you're healing, trying to come back from an injury, you must learn to distinguish between two kinds of pain. Consider this example: At the onset of an injury to a tendon, you feel pain from the trauma to the tendon. After resting for a week, you start rehabilitation exercises. You show steady improvement, until one morning you reach for your cereal bowl and feel a twinge. You think, "Uh oh, I'm still injured." But are you? The pain you felt reaching for the bowl is qualitatively different from the initial pain caused by trauma. This type of pain is the result of nerve entrapment inside the newly formed scar tissue. What happens is that micronerves become trapped inside the repaired tendon tissue, which is less flexible than uninjured tissue. When you reached for your cereal bowl, you stretched that scar tissue, stretching those nerves and sending an electrical surge to your brain.

Here's a good test to determine which kind of pain you are feeling: Do some gentle movements with your injured shoulder, then try reaching for the cereal bowl again. If you feel no pain, it was nerve entrapment the first time. It's okay to work through this kind of pain; in fact, you have to work through it if you expect any improvement.

At the gym, if you warm up slowly with light weights and the pain goes away after several minutes, that's further confirmation that the pain was caused by nerve entrapment. If, however, you add weight too quickly and feel pain well after warming up, it's not nerve entrapment; this type of pain is caused by applying more stress than the injured tendon can handle. Instead of a growth response, you are compounding the trauma. If you apply just the right amount of stress, the injured area gets worked slightly and recuperates stronger.

Overuse injuries, which are the kind you will most commonly face, take a long time to heal, no matter what you do. One time while trying to free-climb the West Face of Sentinel Rock in Yosemite, I was going from one layback to another. I had to reach way up and twist. My feet were really low and starting to slip out. I was straining, with my left arm up by my ear and my shoulder in an awkward, almost dislocated, position. My foot slipped and I fell about 60 feet before I was caught by the belay.

I felt a little tweak in my shoulder but finished the pitch. It ached a little the next climbing day, but I warmed up and felt okay. On the rock, however, I felt it every time I did a strenuous move. By the third or fourth day, I knew something was wrong. Every move began to hurt. I went to a doctor, who put me through resistance exercises to determine which tendon was damaged, then to a physical therapist, who showed me specific exercises to do and how much weight to do them with.

Even with such care, it took me nine months to return to the climbing level I enjoyed before the injury. I was climbing okay after six months but nowhere near 100 percent. Another shoulder injury took fourteen months to heal, and a finger took nine months. In fact, I've never had tendinitis completely heal in less than nine months. Being unable to do what you want to do is so hard—harder than any 5.14 on the planet—that you have to be philosophical about it. Keep in mind that the body will heal itself, that you will eventually climb at 100 percent again.

– 6 –

Ethics

One of climbing's main attractions is its exhilarating freedom. With no rule book, climbers can ascend a route using whatever tactics they like—unless, of course, their methods infringe on the rights of other climbers.

Only in the past couple of decades have climbers descended from a route because it couldn't be free-climbed. Before that, if a party reached such an impasse, they would just aid up and go for the summit. Now, real purists feel that if it can't be done free, it's not worth continuing to the summit. But unfortunately, there don't seem to be enough purists around.

> "All climbers are a product of their first few climbs."
> —Yvon Chouinard

A few years ago, I was invited to a climbing conference in Europe, one purpose of which was to discuss the ethics of climbing. I thought it was going to be great. They paid my way to Germany, which was unheard of then. There were more than five thousand people in attendance, which was also unheard of. In the United States, we'd have drawn maybe five hundred.

But I was disappointed in the discussions on ethics. The speakers saw nothing wrong with starting out at the top of a route and putting in protection so that you could climb safely from the bottom. Of course, everyone makes his own compromises. I realize I'm not as pure as I could be; after all, I use boots and chalk.

Far more ominous than chalk marks, in my opinion, is the growing tendency to physically alter the rock so that people can "free-climb" it. This tendency is especially prevalent in France and, like Christopher Columbus, it has found its way to North America.

The first time I went to climb in France, some French climbers took me to a route called "Rose and the Vampire." Right from the beginning, the holds looked as though they had been improved, maybe with a chisel, but I couldn't be sure. A little higher, I reached up from an undercling but found no hold.

"What do you grab here?" I asked my hosts.

"That little edge in front of you," one of them answered.

All I could see was a piece of rock glued onto the face. "This isn't a hold," I said. "It's been glued onto the rock."

"Mais oui. Because there was no hold there."

Well, that isn't the way I was brought up in the sport. If you can't do a section of rock in its natural state, then the answer is simple: You'd better go home and train some more. Besides, what's to prevent the next climber from gluing a couple more objects onto the rock because he can't even handle the rock you altered? The possible progression is frightening.

It's totally selfish to lower the rock to your level, to conclude that because you can't climb something, you will alter it—whether by chiseling, gluing, or bolting on a hold—so that you can say you free-climbed the route. Aid climbers, of course, alter the rock all the time. They are mainly concerned with reaching the top. But most don't glue on artificial holds, and they don't alter the rock and then claim that they've free-climbed it.

I wish, at the very least, that those French climbers would be honest and call what they do aid climbing. Because that's what it is. Grabbing a stone glued onto the natural rock is no different than grabbing a bolt; it just looks different.

Climbers need to be concerned with two types of ethics. The first kind—*social ethics*—comes into play when you decide to rappel down an intended route, look at all the holds, take pictures, study them at home—all before you climb it. The alternative is to do an on-sight, first-ascent flash—the sport's ultimate challenge—where you climb a route on the first try without falling, with no previous knowledge of its moves. Because ours is a sport with no coaches, no rule book, each climber must make a personal choice. You're your own judge, and if you want to cheapen the sport, you can do so. Of course, it says something about the kind of person you are. If, on the other hand, you like to make it tough on yourself, to establish higher challenges, that's allowed too. Even though I disdain the hangdogging style, the freedom to make your own rules and follow them is one of the reasons I love climbing. You may have different rules, and I support your right to have them. Questions of social ethics will be debated forever.

The second kind—*environmental ethics*—becomes an issue when people physically alter the environment. This goes way beyond merely hangdogging to study a route. It affects other people besides the individual climber. A lot of us resent driving hours to reach nature, only to climb a route and find a glued or chiseled hold. Besides its effect on the athletic event, it's an eyesore. Although one chiseled hold does not by itself destroy the entire environment, it sets a terrible precedent. Some of us like to enjoy the little features as well as the big features.

I believe that you should do as little as possible to alter the environment. Having said that, I admit that I have drilled bolts—every climber has—but I don't do it much, and I try to do it right. That's because I know firsthand what a drag it is to work hard to reach an anchor and find four old chopped bolt studs there. In sharp contrast to the beautiful rock itself, the area has been transformed into an ugly mess.

L imestone, steep with positive holds, is a fun kind of rock to climb, but it is fairly rare in the United States. I recently discovered, however, that Mount Charleston near Las Vegas offers some splendid limestone climbing. It's five hours from my home—almost in my backyard, much easier and cheaper than going to Europe. The problem is, although people have been climbing there for only a few years, most of the holds have been chiseled or filed and there's glue dribbled everywhere. A unique climbing area has been trashed, and all so a few unethical people could do their routes and claim their numbers.

When I first started climbing in the seventies, nuts were just coming on the scene as an alternative to pitons, which were tearing up cracks. There was a big push to do clean ascents, meaning all nuts and no pitons. Then Ray Jardine developed the Friend, a camming device that was very easy to use and did no damage to the rock. So it's ironic that we've reached this state today. After years of realizing that we were screwing up the rock, after all those inventions designed to prevent damage to the rock, now we've come to a point where some climbers intentionally scar the rock. We've gone full circle and beyond.

It's impossible for me to look upon that with approval, but I do try to respect the opinion of the people who do it. Sometimes I wonder, if I were new to the sport, if I hadn't seen all the changes I've seen, would I be a chiseler? . . . Nah.

I'm indebted to the climbers before me who showed me the way, who made possible any success I've had, and who consistently demonstrated high ethical standards. I could have come up with the idea of free climbing on my own, but it's unlikely without predecessors like Yvon Chouinard, Royal Robbins, John Gill, Chuck Pratt, Frank Sacherer, T. M. Herbert, Bob Kamps, and Tom Higgins, to name a few, all of whom had strong preservationist ethics—they believed in leaving the rock in as natural a state as possible. If you look at the climbs they did thirty years ago, you will see that they aren't hacked up. They look just as they did before they were climbed. On the other hand, check out some newer routes—maybe they've been climbed only for a year or so—and it's not uncommon to find chiseled holds and dribbled glue. It's disgusting.

All the rappel sport routes that dot the land really do not have true first ascents. They are all rigged from above, after which the climber boasts that he did a first ascent. In fact, they all have preplaced invisible top ropes in the form of rappel bolts. There is a whole new generation of "me now" climbers whose attitude is that they are going to climb the route any way they can to get their names in a magazine.

What I like to do best is first ascents. That means standing at the bottom of a climb and checking it out with the naked eye. The inner dialogue goes something like this:

"Ah, it looks like I can do it."

"Well, you'll soon find out."

And so I start going up, section by section, and sure enough, I soon find out. It's just the way people used to climb in the old days.

But starting at the top, rappeling down, looking the route over to see if you can do it, putting artificial aids in to ensure that you can, then returning to the base and doing a pseudo first ascent is like getting a copy of the final exam, memorizing it, and then taking the test. In other words, it's cheating. It's not rising to the challenge; it's bringing the challenge down to your level. For me, knowing about a route before I climb it is terrible. It destroys the challenge a climb can offer. I find it sad that so many have adopted this way of thinking.

"There used to be so few climbers that it didn't matter where one drove a piton, there wasn't a worry about demolishing the rock. Now things are different. There are so many of us, and there will be more. A simple equation exists between freedom and numbers; the more people, the less freedom. If we are to retain the beauties of the sport, the fine edge, the challenge, we must consider our style of climbing."

—Royal Robbins

There are routes I've been working on for years, that I'm still working on. Some of them are so hard I may never succeed. There may be a dozen guys in the world who could walk up and do them. But I would never be selfish enough to hack them down to my level.

I hope that this book will encourage you to meet the challenge of the rock. Our climbing resources need to be preserved, and it's up to all of us who love climbing and nature to try to save what we still have.

Behavior on the Rock

- Leave the area as you found it.
- Respect other people's right to enjoy the outdoors in its natural state—even if they aren't climbers.
- Don't leave litter, such as chalk wrappings, old slings, or used adhesive tape.
- Raise yourself to the level of the rock rather than tearing the rock down to your level
- Use restraint with chalk; it gums up holds and looks ugly.
- Don't chisel, glue, or permanently alter the rock.
- Respect local regulations: Routes may be closed because of nesting birds, rare plants, or the danger of falling rock.
- Warn other climbers of imminent danger, such as poor belay or rappel anchors.
- Defecate and urinate away from the rock.

Glossary

abseil: see *rappel*.

accessory cord: thin rope, from 3 to 8 millimeters, often used for making slings and runners.

active rope: the length of rope between a moving climber and the belayer.

aerobic exercise: continuous, rhythmic exercise during which the body's oxygen needs are still being met. Aerobic activities include brisk walking, running, swimming, cycling, and cross-country skiing. A conditioned athlete can carry on aerobic exercise for a long time (in contrast with *anaerobic exercise*).

aid climbing: the technique of moving up a rock face resting on artificial holds. Slings, ropes, nuts, and other paraphernalia are used for physical support, not just for emergency protection or belay anchors (in contrast with *free climbing*).

alternate leads: a method of climbing rock or ice in which two climbers lead alternate pitches of a climb.

anaerobic exercise: exercise at an intensity level that exceeds the ability of the body to dispose of the lactic acid produced by the muscles. As a result, this exercise can be sustained for only a short time before exhaustion sets in. Examples of anaerobic exercise include weight lifting, sprinting, and climbing.

anchor: the point at which a fixed rope, rappel rope, or belay is secured to rock, snow, or ice by any of various means.

angle piton: a metal wedge that is V- or U-shaped in cross section. Designed to fit in cracks from

$^1/_2$ inch wide (*baby angles*) to 4 inches wide (*bongs*). Angle pitons are very stable because they contact the rock in three places.

approach: the distance a climber must hike from the car to the start of the climb. An approach may take anywhere from a few minutes to several days.

arm bar: a means of holding on to a crack in which the open hand presses against one side of the crack and the elbow and upper arm press against the other side.

artificial climbing wall: a climbing surface made out of brick, board, stone, or a mix of polyester resin and sand that has artificial holds for climbers to work out, train, or learn to climb. Many are indoors.

balance climbing: a technique used for climbing smooth rocks whereby a climber maintains a position of balance by careful choice of handholds and footholds.

ballistic stretching: doing quick bouncing stretches that force muscles to lengthen. The muscles react by reflexively contracting or shortening, increasing the likelihood of muscle tears and soreness.

bandolier: a chest loop for carrying climbing equipment.

belay: to tend the climbing rope, ready to immediately put enough friction on the rope to hold the climber in case of a fall. Friction is generated by the rope passing around the belayer's body or through a belay device. Belaying is the primary safeguard in climbing, and its practice is universal. *Belay* also refers to the entire system set up to make belaying possible, including the anchor that holds the belayer in place.

belay device: any of numerous small metal gadgets that force a bend in the climbing rope, creating enough friction to enable a belayer to hold a fall. (See also *descender* and *figure eight*.)

bight: a loop of rope.

big wall: a steep cliff or face, vertical or nearly so, that is 1,000 feet or more from bottom to top.

biner: (pronounced "beaner"): slang for *carabiner*.

body belay: see *waist belay*.

bolt: a thin metal rod that is hammered into a predrilled hole in the rock to serve as a multidirectional anchor. Bolts, ranging in size from $^1/_4$ to $^1/_2$ inch, were originally used to protect free climbers on otherwise unprotectable routes and to piece together crack systems on longer climbs. Because they are left in place for subsequent climbers to use, bolts remain controversial.

bolted route: a route that is entirely protected by bolts.

bolt hanger: a metal piece that is attached to the bolt, allowing a carabiner to be clipped to the bolt.

bombproof: said of a hold or belay that will not fail, regardless of how much weight or force is put on it.

bong: the biggest piton, designed for cracks wider than a person's foot. Also called *bong-bong*.

bouldering: climbing large rocks close to the ground without ropes or protection. Excellent training for big climbs, it has become a sport in its own right.

boulder problem: a route up a boulder. The problem is usually named and rated, and can be top-roped or bouldered.

brake bar: a small aluminum rod that is used to create friction on the rope when a climber is descending by rappel.

bridging: a climbing technique in which the climber pushes out to the sides with hands, feet, or both, using opposing pressure against the rock. Often used in climbing chimneys or dihedrals. Also called *stemming*.

bucket: a large bombproof hold.

bulge: a small overhang.

bumblies: beginners, usually unsupervised, who have no idea what they are doing.

buttress: a section of a mountain or cliff standing out from the rest, often flanked on both sides by gullies or couloirs; somewhat wider than an arête.

carabiner: an oval or D-shaped metal snap-link about 3 inches long in the shape of a giant safety pin. Capable of holding a ton or more, carabiners are used for attaching the rope to anchors in rock or snow.

carabiner brake: a configuration of four to six carabiners arranged to provide rope friction for rappeling.

chalk: light magnesium carbonate, powder or block, used by rock climbers to keep their hands dry and thus improve handholds.

chalk bag: a bag, usually worn at a climber's waist, that holds grip-enhancing chalk.

chest harness: a harness used in conjunction with a waist harness to attach a climber to the rope.

chickenhead: a protruding knob on a rock face that can be used for a hold.

chimney: a crack wide enough to accommodate a climber's entire body.

chimneying: the method of climbing a chimney using the pressure of feet and back on opposing walls.

chock: a rock wedged in a crack or behind a flake, around which a runner can be threaded and then clipped to a rope for an anchor point. Before artificial chocks, British climbers carried pebbles to place in cracks; later they used hexagonal machine nuts found on railroad tracks. Today there are two basic types of chocks: *wedges* and *hexes*. Also called a *chockstone*.

chockcraft: the art of using chocks to create secure anchors in the rock.

chock sling: wire, rope, or webbing that attaches to a chock.

chop: to remove from the rock someone else's protection, such as bolts.

classic routes: ways up mountains that have special character, historical interest, great difficulty, popularity, or a combination of these.

clean climbing: a means of ascension that leaves the rock unscarred and undamaged after the climbing team has passed.

cleaning the pitch: removing all the protection hardware placed by the leader.

cliff: a smooth, steep face of rock.

clip in: to attach oneself to the mountain by means of a carabiner snapped onto an anchor.

clove hitch: one of the two main knots (the other is the figure eight) used in the ropework system.

coiling: the various methods of looping and tying a rope so that it can be carried, all requiring a certain amount of skill to avoid kinking.

corner: an outside junction of two planes of rock, approximately at right angles (in contrast with *dihedral*).

crab: slang for *snap-link carabiner*.

crack: a gap or fracture in the rock, varying in width from a thin seam to a wide chimney.

crag: a low cliff, one or two pitches high.

crux: the most difficult part of a pitch or climb (though some climbs have more than one crux).

deadpoint: the peak of a lunge, when velocity is zero and gravity has not yet started to drag you down.

dehydration: a depletion of body fluids that can hinder the body's ability to regulate its temperature. One can become dehydrated during climbing if the fluids lost from perspiration and respiration are not replaced by drinking water. Chronic dehydration lowers a climber's tolerance to fatigue, reduces his ability to sweat, elevates his rectal temperature, and increases the stress on his circulatory system. In general, a loss of 2 percent or more of one's body weight by sweating affects performance; a loss of 5 to 6 percent affects health.

descender: a friction device used for descending ropes (rappeling). The most common is the figure eight; others include the brake bar and the carabiner brake. Also known as a *rappel device.*

dihedral: a high-angled inside corner where two rock planes intersect; shaped like an open book (in contrast with *corner*).

direct: the most direct way up a route or climb, usually the way water would take to fall down the rock. The direct tends to be steeper and more difficult than ordinary routes.

direct aid: the aid or equipment a climber puts weight on to progress up a rock.

double dyno: two *dynos* in succession.

double up: to anchor two chocks close together for added protection.

down and out: the correct position of a carabiner gate when it is connected to an anchor.

Dulfursitz rappel: method of descending in which a climber threads an anchored climbing rope between his legs, returns it to the front of his body, then wraps it over a shoulder and holds it behind him with one hand.

dyno: a technique for reaching holds that seem just beyond the climber's grasp. The climber sinks slightly, then rises by pushing with the legs and pushing with whatever hand has the current hold, while reaching for the new hold with the other hand. Also called dynamic move.

edging: using the sides of climbing boots to stand on thin rock ledges.

escarpment: an inland cliff formed by the erosion of the inclined strata of hard rocks.

expansion bolt: a bolt that expands and locks when screwed into a prebored hole in the rock. Used when a rock lacks cracks into which a piton or nut can be inserted. Bolts provide the safest protection, but they alter the rock and change the character and degree of difficulty of a climb.

exposed: said of a climber's route that is steep and hard, with a big drop below it.

exposure: a long drop beneath a climber's feet; what one confronts to the max when climbing a sheer face like El Capitan.

extractor: a tool climbers use to remove chocks that have become stuck in cracks. Also called a *chock pick.*

face: a wall of rock steeper than 60 degrees.

face climbing: using handholds and footholds on an open rock face.

face holds: edges and irregularities protruding from a wall, or the pockets sunk into it.

fall factor: a numerical value indicating the severity of a fall. If protection holds, the most serious fall has a value of 2, and most climbing falls are between .5 and 1. Calculate the fall factor by dividing the distance of the fall by the length of rope between you and your belayer.

figure-eight descender: a metal rappeling device in the shape of the numeral 8. One hole is used to attach the device to a harness with a carabiner; a rope is passed through the other hole to provide friction for the descent.

figure-eight knot: one of the two main knots (the other is the clove hitch) used in the ropework system.

finger crack: a crack so thin only a climber's fingers will fit into it.

finger lock: a jam in which the finger is inserted into a crack to obtain a secure anchor point.

first ascent: the first time a route has been climbed.

fist crack: a crack the size of a fist.

fist jam: a secure but painful (for the beginner) way of finding a purchase on a rock. In a fist jam, the climber shoves his hand into a gap in the rock and makes a fist, swelling the hand for use as an anchor point. The thumb is pushed into the palm to stretch the skin and create a wider profile.

fixed protection: anchors, such as bolts or pitons, that are permanently placed in the rock.

fixed rope: a rope that a climber has anchored and left in place after a pitch is climbed so that climbers can ascend and descend at will. Most expedition climbing uses fixed ropes to facilitate load carrying and fast retreat over dangerous terrain.

flake: a thin, partly detached leaf of rock. Also, to prepare a rope so that it won't tangle when you are using it.

flapper: torn skin on the hand—the kind that flaps.

flaring crack: a crack with sides that flare out.

flash: to climb a route on the first try, without falling or hanging from the rope. Many consider it the best style.

free climbing: climbing in which natural handholds and footholds are used. Hardware is used only for protection and not for support or progress (in contrast with *aid climbing*).

free soloing: climbing without partners, equipment, and (usually) ropes.

French free: resting on protection while otherwise free climbing.

friction brake: a device that provides rope friction when rappeling, such as a bar mounted on one or more carabiners.

friction climbing: ascending slabs using friction between shoes and rock or hands and rock, instead of distinct holds.

Friend: an active (spring-loaded) camming device inserted into a crack as an anchor point. Designed and marketed by Ray Jardine in 1978, the Friend was a major breakthrough because it allowed climbers to protect roofs and parallel cracks with minimal time spent making the placement.

frost wedging: the opening and widening of a crack by the repeated freezing and thawing of ice in the crack.

gardening: cleaning a climb of vegetation and loose rocks.

gear freak: a climber who has lots of equipment but not much knowledge.

glacial erratic: a boulder transported by a glacier from its original source.

glacial groove: a deep, straight scratch on a rock surface caused by the movement of sediment-laden glaciers over bedrock.

glacial striation: a straight scratch on a rock surface, only a few millimeters deep, caused by the movement of sediment-laden glaciers.

glacis: an easy-angled slab of rock between horizontal and 30 degrees. A slab is steeper, and a wall steeper yet.

gripped: said of a climber who is paralyzed with fear.

groove: a shallow, vertical crack.

gully: steep-sided rift or chasm, deep and wide enough to walk inside.

Gunkie: a climber who favors the Shawangunks, a famous escarpment in New York.

hand traverse: horizontal movement across a rock face in which the body is supported mainly by the hands.

hangdogging: hanging on a rope, either after a fall or to study a route.

hanging belay: a belay station on vertical rock that offers no ledge for support.

harness: a contraption worn around the shoulders or waist, usually made of wide tape, and offering convenient loops through which to clip a climber's rope and gear. If a climber falls while roped onto a harness, the shock load is distributed over a wide area. The climber also has a better chance of remaining in an upright position, lowering the risk of his head meeting rock.

haul bag: a bag used for holding and hauling gear up a wall.

hawser-laid rope: rope made from three groups of filaments plaited together.

headlamp: a light that is mounted on a climber's helmet or headband.

headwall: the sheerest, often most difficult, section of a cliff or mountain, usually its uppermost.

hero loop: see *tie-off loop*.

hip belay: see *waist belay*.

hold: a protrusion or indentation in the rock that a climber can grasp with fingers (handhold) or stand on (foothold).

horn: a protruding piece of rock over which a sling can be hung for an anchor.

ice piton: a piton designed to be hammered into ice.

ice screw: a threaded metal device with a pointed tip that is pounded, then screwed, into hard ice. It serves the same purpose as a piton in rock.

impact force: the tug a falling climber feels from the rope as it stops a fall.

inactive rope: rope between any two climbers who are not moving.

isometric exercise: exercise not associated with movement, such as a fingertip hang.

isotonic exercise: exercise associated with movement, such as a pull-up.

jam crack: a gap in the rock that offers inadequate handholds but is wide enough for the climber to find purchase by inserting fingers, hand, fist, or feet.

jamming: wedging fingers, hand, fist, or feet into a crack to create an anchor point.

jug: a large, indented hold; a type of *bucket*.

kernmantle: standard climbing rope in which a core (kern), constructed of one or more braided units, is protected by an outer braided sheath (mantle).

knee jam (lock): a jam in which the knee is inserted into a perfect-sized crack and flexed to create a secure anchor point.

knife blade: a long, thin piton.

laybacking: Grabbing a vertical edge, often a flake of rock, then pulling with hands, pushing with feet, and walking the feet up almost alongside the hands. It is a strenuous but useful technique for arêtes, corners with cracks, and cracks offset in walls. Also called *liebacking*.

lead: the first climber in a party of roped climbers; the head of an expedition. Also called the *leader*.

leader fall: a fall taken by the lead climber. The leader will fall double whatever the distance is to the closest protection.

leading through: said of a second climber continuing to climb through a stance, thereby becoming the leader. If both climbers are of more or less equal competence, this is an efficient way to climb.

ledge: a level area on a cliff or mountain; may be grass, rock, or snow.

load capacity: the maximum load that a piece of gear can withstand.

manteling: a technique in which the

climber moves up high enough to push down on a ledge with both hands until the body is supported on stiffened arms. The climber then replaces one hand with a high-stepping foot and moves up to stand on the ledge.

mixed route: a route involving both rock climbing and ice-and-snow climbing.

multidirectional anchor: an anchor that is secure no matter which direction a load comes from. Bolts, some fixed pitons, and some chock configurations are multidirectional anchors.

multipitch route: a climb consisting of more than one pitch.

nailing: hammering a chain of pitons into a crack.

natural anchor: a tree, boulder, or other natural feature that is well placed and strong enough to make a good anchor.

natural line: a rock climb that follows an obvious feature up the face of a cliff, such as a groove, gully, or series of cracks.

niche: a small recess in a rock face, usually large enough to hold a climber.

nose: a jutting protrusion of rock, broad and sometimes with an undercut base.

nut: an artificial chockstone, usually made of aluminum alloy and threaded with nylon cord. Nuts are fitted into cracks in the rock and usually can be used in place of pitons, which can scar the rock. A climber using only nuts needs no hammer, since nuts can be lifted out of their placements.

objective dangers: mountain hazards that are not necessarily the result of flaws in a climber's technique. They include avalanches, rockfall, and crevasses.

off-finger crack: a crack too wide to finger-jam, but too narrow to hand-jam.

off-hand jam: a crack too wide to hand-jam, but too narrow to fist-jam.

off-width: a crack too wide to fist-jam, but too narrow to fit the whole body into.

off-width protection: chocks that are wide enough to anchor in an off-width.

on-sight: to climb a route with no previous knowledge of its moves.

on-sight flash: to climb a route on the first try without falling and with no previous knowledge of its moves.

open book: a high-angled inside rock corner; a *dihedral*.

opposing chock: a chock that is anchored in the opposite direction from another chock. In combination, the two chocks protect against a multidirectional load.

overdriven: said of a piton when its effectiveness is reduced by too much hammering.

overhang: rock that exceeds 90 degrees.

overuse injury: tissue damage caused by doing too much too fast (in contrast with *traumatic injury*).

palming: a friction hold in which a climber presses the palm of the hand into the rock.

pedestal: a flat-topped, detached pinnacle.

peg: the British term for *piton*.

Perlon: German trade name for a plastic similar to nylon.

pin: see *piton*.

pinkpoint: to lead a climb without falling or resting on aid while clipping the rope to preplaced protection (compare with *redpoint*). The leader may have previously attempted the route.

pinnacle: a partially detached feature, like a church steeple.

pitch: a section of climbing between two stances or belay points, usually the length of a 150- or 165-foot rope. It is the farthest the leader will go before allowing the second on the rope to catch up.

piton: a metal wedge hammered into a crack until it is secure, used as an anchor point for protection or aid. In the United States, pitons are used only when absolutely necessary, because repeated use damages rock. The first hard-steel pitons were made by John Salathé for use on the Southwest Face of Half Dome in 1946. Also called *pin* or *peg*.

piton hammer: a hammer designed and carried for pounding in and extracting pitons.

piton scar: a groove in the rock caused by the placement and removal of a piton.

pocket: a shallow hole—and thus hold—in the rock.

pooling: a method of rope management in which the climber places one end of the rope on the ground and piles concentric loops of rope on top.

Portaledge: a cotlike sleeping platform, suspended on a vertical rock face from pitons.

power: strength-to-weight ratio, and thus not simply dependent on size of muscles.

pressure hold: a foothold or handhold used to maintain a position on a rock face by exerting pressure sideways and downward on it.

protection: the anchors—such as chocks, bolts, or pitons—to which a climber connects the rope while ascending.

protection system: the configuration of anchors, runners, carabiners, ropes, harnesses, and belayer that combine to stop a falling climber.

prow: a rock feature resembling the prow of a ship, such as the Nose of El Capitan.

prusik: a technique for climbing a rope, originally by use of a prusik knot, now also by means of mechanical ascenders. The knot, invented by Karl Prusik, uses a loop of thin rope wound around a larger-diameter rope in such a way that the knot will slide freely when unweighted but will grip tightly to the main rope when a climber's weight is applied to it.

put up: to make the first ascent of a route.

rack: the collection of climbing gear carried by the lead climber, as arranged on a gear sling. Also, to arrange the gear on the sling.

rappel: to descend by sliding down a rope. Friction for controlling the descent is provided by wraps of rope around the body or by a mechanical rappel device. The rope is usually doubled so that it can be pulled down afterward. Also called *abseil*.

rappel device: see *descender*.

rappel point: the anchor for a rappel—that is, what the rope, or the sling holding it, is fastened to at the top.

rating systems: a system of terms or numbers describing the difficulty of climbs. There are seven major rating systems, including the American (Yosemite) Decimal, British, French, East German, and Australian systems.

rat tail: an excessively worn, unsafe climbing rope.

redpoint: to lead a climb without falling or resting on aid, and while placing protection as the climb is made. A redpoint may occur after the climber has practiced the route.

rock-climbing boots: soft boots with flat rubber soles designed to grip rock.

roof: an overhanging section of rock that is close to horizontal. Roofs vary in size from an eave of a few centimeters to giant cantilevers several yards wide.

rope: important element of the belay system. Modern climbing rope is 150 or 165 feet of nylon kernmantle. Lead ropes range from 10 to 12 millimeters in diameter, backup ropes 8 to 9 millimeters. According to John Forrest Gregory in *Rock Sport*, the ideal climbing rope would have all the following qualities: low impact force, low elongation under both impact force and low load, good handling qualities, light weight, water resistance, high ratings for holding falls, resistance to cutting and abrasion, and a low price.

roped solo climbing: free-climbing or aid-climbing a route alone but protected by a rope. An advanced technique, requiring a lot of gear.

roping up: the act of a party of climbers tying themselves together with climbing ropes.

route: a particular way up a cliff. A cliff may have dozens of routes, each with a name and rating.

runner: a short length of nylon webbing or accessory cord tied or stitched to form a loop; used for connecting anchors to the rope and for other climbing applications. Also called a *sling*.

runout: a section of a climb that is unprotectable, other than with bolts (which may be discouraged).

rurp: an acronym for Realized Ultimate Reality Piton, the smallest piton in the arsenal. A rurp, about the size of a postage stamp, fits into a fingernail-thick crack.

safety margin: the amount of extra strength built into climbing gear. For example, a carabiner may have a strength rating of 6,000 pounds, but it rarely has to support more than 3,000 pounds. Thus it has a safety margin of 3,000 pounds.

sandbagging: misrepresenting the difficulty of a climb, rating it easier than it really is.

scoop: an indentation in the rock face, not as deep as a niche.

scramble: an easy climb, usually without a rope (in contrast with *technical climbing*).

scree: a long slope of loose stones on a mountainside.

screwgate: a carabiner that can be "locked" with a barrel on a screw thread. Less common than snap-links, screwgates are used when there is a risk that the gate will open. Also called a *locking carabiner*.

seam: a crack far too thin for fingers but big enough to accept some small chocks, pitons, or copperheads.

second: the climber who follows the lead. Though the lead might take a substantial fall, the second usually risks only a short fall, as the belay is from above. The second usually cleans the pitch.

self-belay: the technique of protecting oneself during a roped solo climb, often with a self-belay device.

sewing-machine leg: violent shaking in the leg resulting from holding a bent-knee position too long.

sit bag: a cloth seat that climbers attach to the rock and sit in to make hanging from a wall more comfortable.

slab: large, smooth rock face inclined between 30 and 60 degrees.

sling: see *runner*.

smearing: a technique of friction

climbing used on steep, scooped holds, where the sole of the boot is squashed into the depression to gain the best hold.

snap-link: a carabiner with a spring-loaded gate that opens inward (in contrast with *screwgate*).

soloing: climbing alone, whether roped or unroped, aided or free.

spike: a finger of rock.

sport rappeling: descending a rope in a fast, bouncy manner, with speed as the main goal.

stance: the position a climber is in at any given time, especially the position of the belayer.

static move: a climbing move in which at least two points of contact (e.g, a hand and a foot) remain in contact with the rock (in contrast with *dyno*).

stemming: see *bridging*.

stopper: a wedge-shaped nut.

swami belt: part of the harness; 10 to 12 feet of 1- or 2-inch webbing wrapped around the waist in such a way that allows a climber to tie on to it with a rope.

taking in: removing slack in the active rope from a moving climber.

talus: the weathered rock fragments that accumulate at the base of a slope.

technical climbing: climbing that requires hardware, harnesses, ropes, and specialized climbing boots (in contrast with a *scramble*).

third-classing: free-soloing a Class 4 or Class 5 route without protection.

tie-off loop: a short loop of nylon webbing tied to a piton near the rock to reduce leverage.

tincture of benzoin: a solution of water, alcohol, and benzoin (resin from a tree in Java) that climbers can apply to their hands to provide a protective coating against rock abrasion.

toe hooking: a climbing technique in which a toe is hooked around a rock edge.

top rope: a rope anchored above a climber, providing maximum security; sometimes called *TR*. To *top-rope* means to rig a climb with a top rope or to climb a pitch using a top rope.

traumatic injury: tissue damage that results from a sudden overload or severe impact, such as the body hitting the ground after a fall.

traverse: to proceed around rather than straight over an obstacle; to climb from side to side. A traverse may be an easy walk along a ledge or a daunting passage. Protecting traverses is often difficult, because a fall will cause the climber to pendulum, ending up off route even if no injuries occur.

tunnel vision: seeing only a small area directly in front. This is a

common pitfall for the beginning climber, who, because of
nervousness, may miss an obvious hold that is nearby but off
to one side.

undercling: a hold that permits the
climber to grip the rock from
below with the palms up.

unidirectional anchor: an anchor
that will hold securely if loaded
from one direction but will pull
free if loaded from any other
direction.

waist belay: a method of taking in
and paying out a belayed active
rope. The belayer passes the
rope around his waist; the hand
on the active rope side is the
directing hand, and the hand on
the slack rope side is the *braking
hand*. Also called *hip belay* or
body belay.

wall: a steep cliff or face, between 60
and 90 degrees.

windchill: the cooling of the body
that results from wind passing
over its surface, especially dra-
matic if the surface is wet. It is a
more useful measurement of
meteorological discomfort than
temperature alone.

zipper: a series of poor anchor placements, all of which can be
expected to pop out, one after
the other, if the leader takes a
fall.